TWIN FLAME

WILLIAM R. FORSTCHEN

and

NORA D'ECCLESIS

Copyright © 2017 by Backyard Siblings, LLC

Cover image: © Can Stock Photo / Irochka

All rights reserved, including the right to reproduce this book or portions thereof in any form.

Table of Contents

Introduction by William R. Forstchen

Introduction by Nora D'Ecclesis

Chapter One, In the Beginning	1
Chapter One Narration: The Opening of the Heart	19
Chapter Two, I'd Like to Get to Know You…	23
Chapter Two Narration: Initial Encounter	37
Chapter Three, Let the Courtship Begin!	41
Chapter Three Narration: Synchronicity	55
Chapter Four, Some Back Story	59
Chapter Four Narration: Escaping the Early Relationships as a Learning Process	73
Chapter Five, Memories of Dating Past	77
Chapter Five Narration: Learning toward Communication Skills	95
Chapter Six, The First Thanksgiving…Time to Meet the Family	99
Chapter Six Narration: Root Chakra	125
Chapter Seven, The Time of Troubles	129
Chapter Seven Narration: Disharmony	155
Chapter Eight, Getting Married	157
Chapter Eight Narration: "Katallasso"	165
Conclusion	169
About William R. Forstchen	171
Books by William R. Forstchen	172
About Nora D'Ecclesis	173
Books by Nora D'Ecclesis	174

Introduction to *Twin Flame*
by William R. Forstchen

If you are one of those readers who not only takes time to actually read an introduction to a book, but beyond that, check out the copyright page you might note that this book is copyrighted by Backyard Siblings, LLC.

Why such a curious company name? You see, it is this way. Professionally I am referred to as Dr. Forstchen, and the other author of this book, who provides the twin flame analysis and commentary, is Nora D'Ecclesis. But to each other we are Billy and Nora Lee. We grew up in a working class neighborhood in northern New Jersey, a neighborhood of row homes inhabited by immigrants and first-generation Americans. Me, a German/Irish kid, Nora, Italian. We were literally backyard neighbors.

When did we get to know each other? Neither of us can remember, though there is a legendary photo of us sunbathing "au natural," our mothers sitting to either side and smiling, we too young yet to be embarrassed. An earliest memory for me is of the last great polio scare, I believe it was 1954, when half a dozen kids in our neighborhood were stricken. Our mothers quarantined us except for one playmate that summer, each other, and thus we bonded deeply. A bond that now extends across more than six decades.

We shared all, good and bad, growing up. As teens we were tossed into a less-than-friendly regional junior high and high school. Until then the world of working class folks was all we knew. What an education those next few years were at the hands of the nouveau rich snobs who judged all by clothing and luxury cars! Allowances for fourteen-year-olds often exceeded what our mothers had each week to feed an entire family. The darker side of some of those experiences bonded us even closer.

We weathered those storms, I moved to another town at seventeen, college came, and we drifted apart sometimes. But always, like a lodestone, something: a happy moment, a crisis, a time when you need your childhood friend whom you trust without reservation, would draw us back together.

And thus it was four or so years back when the topic first started to come up about writing a book together. We found it ironic that, out of our little working class neighborhood, so scorned by those who literally lived on the other side of the tracks, from our little circle of acquaintances most had gone on to higher educations, Ph.Ds, and, at least three of us, becoming successful authors. Perhaps something to take note of that the values of traditional working class communities can indeed be the breeding ground for stability and success.

Ideas morphed around across a couple of years concerning what to write about, and then this one hit. To reveal the personal, I had endured a tragic, sad divorce half a decade earlier and then met the woman who would indeed be the fulfillment of that long cherished, near-mythical concept of a twin flame relationship. Nora saw it clearly, was the first to say "Billy this is it, you've found your Twin Flame," and urged that we write about it. When a time came that, for a variety of reasons, the twin flame nearly flickered out, it was Nora who, with steady quiet counseling, was crucial in keeping the belief in that flame alive and helping to fan it back to brilliant intensity.

That is the story about how a journey started in infancy is today the book you are about to read.

William R. Forstchen
May 17, 2017

Introduction to *Twin Flame*
By Nora D'Ecclesis

My dear friend Bill Forstchen has been a huge part of my life since we were toddlers. I am in awe of his accomplishments as a novelist and incredibly proud of all aspects of the work he does, including those late night radio interviews!

Billy is the friend who walked me to school when we were four and took my hand when I started to cry leaving home. (Actually he was four and I was tad older!) We were neighbors and our parents were close friends.

As kids, Billy explained the Cuban missile crisis to me as we played badminton in my yard and later that evening his dad helped us produce a Civil War reenactment with action figures in his home to distract us from the danger.

Billy and I hugged and prayed when he lost his granddad and later on, then my dad. We pledged our friendship and loyalty to each other with a ceremonial mingling of blood drops on our fingers.

As a former educator and member of a board of education it has always been my hope that the informational nature of my work benefits more people than could be reached with seminars and retreats. For that, I thank Bill for suggesting years ago that I publish.

Billy is my brother. Over the years we have kept in touch with family vacations, Skype and lots of phone calls. Bill stood at my marriage after vetting my husband and, five decades later, he and my husband are still great friends. I supported Bill through the tribulations of his own twin flame process.

Billy and I are backyard siblings.

Bill and I have co-authored this novel with great joy,

drawing on our own areas of expertise. It is an honor to write with Bill, who is one of the greatest novelists I have ever read. Bill and I spent many hours discussing Samuel Taylor Coleridge's meaning of a soul mate and decided to kick it up a notch to a definitive look at the newer holistic concept of twin flame. Twin Flame is a book about the loving relationship between a husband and wife. The end result is a work interwoven with expert novelization and the holistic concept of the twin flame process.

> "To be happy in married life…you must have a soul mate."
> Samuel Taylor Coleridge,
> *A Letter to a Young Lady* (1822)

Nora D'Ecclesis
May 5, 2017

TWIN FLAME

WILLIAM R. FORSTCHEN
and
NORA D'ECCLESIS

Chapter One
~
In the Beginning

November 2, 2013. I guess for 99.9% of the world it was the most ordinary of days. If remembered, maybe it was because it was a day of marrying or birthing for someone you know, or a day of dying. It usually takes something like that to remember a specific date years later. But for nearly all of us, you know how it is. You get up, think about what plans you have, maybe with anticipation, maybe with happiness, at times with sadness, or even with a touch of dread of, "Oh no, I've got to do such and such today." The day passes, another one of what you hope are still thousands to come, and memory of it fades with time.

If you've ever seen Thorton Wilder's *Our Town*, I suspect the final act is etched into your memory as it is into mine. Remember it? Emily is dead and she asks God (who in the play is called the Stage Manager) if she can go back and relive a day in her life. He allows her go back to observe what he defines as a "most ordinary of days."

And she is overwhelmed.

For the first time, she sees how remarkable, how beautifully stunning a most ordinary day in our lives can actually be. The "Stage Manager" lets her journey back ten years. Emily is again fourteen years old, standing in her family's kitchen. She watches her mother preparing breakfast, sees her father coming home from a meeting, observes the most mundane and trivial details of the milkman on his morning rounds, smells the scent of breakfast cooking, and relives the memory of a warm bed on a cold winter day, the gate in her front yard, and her favorite tree. It is all there before her a most "ordinary of days" when she was fourteen. She is transfixed, filled with awe and then sorrow at all that life was that she had not embraced while still alive. She finally cries out to "God," saying that it is all so beautiful and asking, "Do we ever see, while alive, just how beautiful life can truly be?"

He slowly shakes his head, sighs, and says "No." But then he pauses and, with a wistful smile, answers, "Saints and poets maybe … they do some."

Saints and poets: the ones who see the moments of life that are truly sublime. That is what this book is about, for when you find your twin flame, life can truly be sublime and you try to learn to embrace, every single day, the beauty of what life truly is. If you are so blessed, from time to time you will know what it is like to be a "saint or poet."

When I awoke that morning of November 2, 2013, I did not know that it would become the most important day of my life, one that in my heart and memory I have revisited every day since, recalling each detail with warmth. If, after I leave this earth, the "Stage Manager" allows me to go back to one day in particular it will be that day.

It was a Saturday, normally a day of the week that I'd sleep in until nine or ten before crawling out of bed and, half awake, struggle to make a cup of coffee before wandering into my office.

I have a great career; I am an author and college professor. The old statement that if you love your job you'll never work a day in your life is true, but there are times it can still be tedious. A typical day in that year of 2013 was filled with writing and editing a lengthy novel that, at times, was a real brain drainer when it came to research and fact checking.

Along with the writing there is the marketing side of

life as an author. If you are going to survive in the publishing world, then marketing, doing radio interviews, attending conferences, and giving speeches is part of the game. This particular morning it was giving a speech.

I enjoy public speaking. I grew up a very nerdy, uncoordinated and unathletic kid who had yet to be diagnosed with dyslexia. My junior year in high school I was expelled from a Catholic monastic school (that was another one of the best days of my life!) and tossed into a public school for my senior year. Yeah, that was one of the greatest blessings of my life, the day that I landed on the doorstep of Hightstown High School, Hightstown, New Jersey. A day that shaped the trajectory of my life, which finally led me to the blessing of November 2, 2013, forty-five years later.

A history teacher at that high school, seeing my fascination for the Civil War era, put me up in front of his class for a couple of weeks to take over teaching about the battles of that war. He unlocked a door. There was indeed something that I could do rather well: stand on my feet and talk. Later that year a drama teacher cast me in a spring musical where I had to stand before a thousand and sing ... and I loved it.

I found something of myself when up on that stage or in front of a classroom, but the irony of it is, I am a natural born introvert. I love giving a speech; I've taught in front of a classroom for over thirty years, given talks to thousands, and have even done live national television. But before and after, my stomach is in a knot.

Thus it was that morning of November 2nd. I got up early, showered, shaved, and, nerd-like, did not comb my hair (until after that day), then drove sixty miles to a mountain conference center to give a one-hour talk about a book that I had written several years ago.

TWIN FLAME

Frankly I would have preferred another day of solitude: hang around the house, read, or indulge my big passion in life, flying an antique World War II-era airplane, for the air that morning was clear and calm, though there was a forecast for storms by mid-day.

No, I had promised a friend, the organizer of the conference, that I would show up and give a talk and she had slotted me in as the keynote speaker. On such mornings I often toy with the idea of putting on a gravelly voice and calling in sick. How different my life would be now if I had done so that day.

The conference center is a beautiful place, tucked into the high mountains of western North Carolina. Their large auditorium is identical to the one at the college campus where I teach, a vast twelve-sided structure, built of local rock back in the 1920s, the walls studded with mica that shimmers and glows in the sunlight.

As I crossed the narrow one-lane bridge into the conference center I could see that the parking lot was packed and I felt a slight inner shiver … a thousand or more would be there. I actually do enjoy meeting people but after I give a one-hour talk to a large audience, the tough part comes: hand-shaking, signing books, and chatting, which is something with which I feel awkward. I am so appreciative of folks who want to chat with me, and I give it my all, but afterwards I am completely drained. I still smoked cigarettes then so after parking my car I paced around the parking lot and chain smoked a couple before heading into the hall.

I actually do believe in guardian angels. When you've gone through some extremely hellish and frightening moments in your life and in those moments you hear an inner voice whispering calming words, or directing you what to do next, I believe that is an angel on your shoulder. I recall a car accident when I was twenty that could have killed me, and, seconds before it unfolded, something told me to put on my seat belt. That something was a guardian angel, a voice of warning. Seconds later a woman in a huge Buick ran a stop sign in front of my VW bug. I'd find out later that I was just the latest in a number of her victims of reckless driving. In that last second something guided me to an impact that, though injured, I could at least hobble away from. I will never forget the first police officer on the scene, surveying the wreck, who knelt down by my side to tell me an ambulance was on the way, asked if I had been wearing a seat belt and when I said yes he replied, "You're lucky kid, if you hadn't, you'd be dead now."

Guardian angels are real!

I learned to believe in them that day and as I write this they are part of the narrative.

As I look back at that moment on November 2, 2013, chain smoking cigarettes in the parking lot, nerving myself to go in and give another speech, I can now imagine my guardian angels holding a final briefing above me.

My guardian angels? Not little bare-butted cherubs with wings. I see mine as a bit of a grizzled bunch, needing a shave, a bit of a battle-weary look in their eyes, given so many of the follies of my life up until then. Perhaps the staff sergeant leading the bunch wears a battered kepi hat out of the Civil War and perpetually chews on a cigar. That's how I see my guardian angels, definitely not out of some baroque painting by Reubens. Those paintings always crack me up. Here is some guy trying to make time with a woman (usually scantily clad and very overweight), while overhead half a dozen naked babies are flying around. Anyone who has ever changed a baby's diaper knows the folly of holding a bare-butt kid, especially a boy, directly over your head! My guardian angels definitely have pants on, and they were out in force on that "day of days."

A bit of a final nervous briefing might have been going on with my "staff sergeant" angel running down the check list:

"Okay guys, this is it! He's showered, shaved. Damn it why can't we get him to comb his hair? Everyone synchronize your watches and be ready to move. I want eye contact, a good smile, kill the tired look and suppress the urge to sit there like an idiot, tongue-tied and looking like a goggle-eyed fish out of water when the Big Moment comes!"

(Nods all around from the assistant guardians as they check their watches and mutter agreement. Of course I know nothing of this, one doesn't actually hear guardian angels except in the rarest of moments!)

"Now listen up people!" the sergeant continues. I've just put in a radio check to the other team. They're reporting some hesitation, something about bailing out early and leaving but they are pushing this plan through. We've worked on it for years. This is the big one. It is now or never! You've got to make sure he does this right the moment he walks out there! Now let's not screw this up! This is it!"

All of this is going on above me while I nervously stare at the conference center, check my own watch, and see that I've got twenty minutes before I go up on stage. I grind out the cigarette and force a smile, inwardly thinking that I can give the talk, hang around for an hour or so to chat with folks, and then flee for home within a couple of hours.

Coming into the conference hall the organizers are waiting for me, all smiles. They are indeed darn good friends as they enthusiastically greet me, pointing to the crowd in the auditorium where someone is giving a talk on some aspect of prepping. I really can't remember now what it was. The minutes tick down, the speaker wraps it up, one of the staff leads me to the foot of the stage, steps up to the podium and begins my introduction.

It is always a bit humbling and even a tad embarrassing to be introduced. Years earlier I had written a novel. I don't like the term "post apocalypse," but unfortunately that is what the novel falls under. I wrote the book as a warning of how fragile our national infrastructure truly is, and if one key component fails we will be in for a terrible time of it.

To my disbelief, (and that of many a critic) within days of the release, the book turned into a *New York Times* best seller and some people claim that it played a key role in helping to launch what is called the "prepper movement." Across my career I've written over forty books, ranging from my start in science fiction to traditional history and historical fiction. What happened when that book came out was a foray into a whole new realm. I was suddenly a best-selling author and it is still a shock to walk into a room and there are a six hundred or more folks wanting to hear what I have to say. In contrast I will always recall my first "autograph party," where not a single soul showed up, and for years, if a dozen were waiting for me at a book signing, that was a success!

So as one of the conference organizers was building me up with his introduction, I was looking around at the audience. All of us have sat through innumerable classes in high school or college where the second hand on that big clock behind the speaker seems frozen. It is the same with conferences and I've tried to master the technique of making that clock move quickly for an audience.

TWIN FLAME

There was a round of applause as I approached the podium and a moment's nervous hesitation as I looked out at the audience. When you've talked about the same subject a hundred times or more you start to develop sound bites to string together. A big thing for me, I hate Powerpoint presentations! Especially the ones where the speaker puts a slide up and then reads it to you. Ugh!

I tend to teach my college classes from memory. After you've taught the same subject fifteen to twenty times it just falls into place. And besides, I teach history, it is not as if the entire subject needs an update every two to three years. I like the spontaneity of teaching that way and one never knows the direction it might take for an hour or so. It is the same when giving an hour-long speech. I might scribble a few notes on a slip of paper which I pull out of my pocket as I start and that is it. As I looked at that audience (and remember those guardian angels are sweating now because Operation Twin Flame is less than an hour away), I tried to judge them. Who were they? Did they want me to just talk about my book, or talk about prepping and how to go about it? In nearly all situations my routine is to make a few quick comments about why I wrote the book and then get the audience involved with question and answers.

As I nervously scanned at the audience I could sense the majority of folks out there had heard me before and that was my first comment: a question asking how many had read my book? In response nearly every hand went up.

Okay, chuck the standard talk about the book. Fallback position? "Let's just make this question and answer since you guys have heard me drone on before." I could see a lot of smiles from the audience and a second later a score of hands were raised.

So thus it was for the next hour. Though there must

have been six hundred or so out there, it felt like a fun college seminar roundtable. Some questions were personal, mention of my daughter who was twenty at the time and a junior at Chapel Hill, some about the book, others about politics which I try to steer away from other than reference to my frustration about the failure of our government, federal and state, to react to the problems presented in my book. There were even some highly technical questions which when stumped I readily admitted my ignorance and asked if someone in the audience knew the answer. (My guardian angels loved that response and would report later it had won me many points!)

The hour ran down. I could see the moderator give me the signal that I was into my last few minutes and I wrapped up as I almost always do with a quote from my hero Abraham Lincoln about our need as a nation to transcend the crisis of the moment and to "think anew and act anew."

I felt it was a good ending, and dang did I need a cigarette! I thanked the audience then headed backstage to what they call in the business the "green room." I shook hands with the organizers who told me folks were starting to line up for book autographs. I hate to keep people waiting but begged off for "just five minutes" so I could down a soda and slip outside for, you got it, a cigarette.

Cigarettes. Yeah I'm an idiot ever since a childhood friend lured me out to a hidden corner of our adjoining backyards and produced a pack of Winstons. She even had some spray mouthwash ready for afterwards and I was hooked. It has been an on and off struggle my entire life. I even quit once for a couple of years when in the running for the Teacher Astronaut program, only to get bumped from that, fortunately, due to local politics and the teacher's union in Maine. I was just lucky though, given the tragic end results. In one of my novels, the addiction is a subplot for the main character trying to quit, and stay that way, across three books.

So I puffed one down, chugged a Pepsi (another addiction), took a few deep breaths, and walked back out onto the stage.

It was X minus seventeen minutes and counting.

A line of at least fifty or more people were waiting to have books signed. Yet again, I can too easily recall at the start of my writing career where not one person, zero, zilch, showed up! So to see so many who actually wanted me to sign a book was a great compliment. I went over to where the organizers had set up a table on the stage, pulled out my trusty Sharpie pen, and got to it.

I've stood on more than a few autograph lines myself. There is something about meeting an author who relates to you to the point that you actually want him to sign one of his books. You wish you could have fifteen, twenty minutes just one-on-one to talk. But always there is a line behind you and rarely more than a moment to say thank you, shake hands, and move on. Also, most authors are, in reality, rather reclusive people. Think about it. Contrary to crummy Hollywood fantasies that we all have upscale beach houses with a spotless office and, at day's end, after laboring over a few hundred words, it is off to a crazed night life. No, the vast majority of us labor alone, in cluttered, often smelly offices, immersed in what we are trying to imagine and bring to life. After doing that, to go out and be the life of the party, or to be super entertaining at a conference is a stretch. I've seen some authors behave that way, and frankly I found most who do to have huge ego issues or are "posers."

Don't get me wrong, nearly all authors enjoy meeting

fans, but when overwhelmed by fifty to a hundred who want to talk it can be a bit taxing.

When on the receiving end as I now was, it is a strange feeling. Most folks are delighted, want to share a quick anecdote, and if it is a kid, or someone military or ex-military I always want to take an extra minute or two to say thank you and add something personal to the autograph rather than just a signature.

Now, there are a few though, where it gets uncomfortable. There are the ones who really want to gab, but after a few minutes, I look behind that person and I see the crowd getting impatient. I should add an extra personal detail here. I'm dyslexic and have some problems with social skills at times. I've never been one to mix at a party or event, small talk a minute, then move on to the next and then the next. So it is awkward for me to ask the "gabber" to please move on and we'll try and catch up the conversation later.

Every once in awhile it just gets strange. At one event, fortunately those running it had hired professional security, a woman had to be dragged away when she started yelling that my book upset her. At another one I actually got slugged by a woman who could have passed as a sumo wrestler. She actually busted my lip open, knocked me over and was ready to do a professional wrestling stomp on me before security intervened and pulled her away. You never know what is going to happen! And little did I know my guardian angels were anxiously watching the line, on the phone with the other team of guardian angels to hang on, just a few more minutes to go!

The line slowly moved along; usually it takes a minute or so for each person. Somebody came up, I have vague recollection she had several books to give to friends as gifts and of course I personalized each. Meanwhile, hovering above me, my chief guardian angel was looking at his watch, scanning the line, only one more person to go, looking over at "the one." Her guardian angels were nervously shepherding her along, stilling any thoughts she might have of just skipping the line and leaving for home. One more to go, my angel now doing the countdown ...

X minus fifteen seconds and counting ... we are at ten, nine, eight...!

The woman with the three or four books stepped aside, I offered a smile and a thank you, and turned my attention to the next person in line.

I've been a writer for over thirty-five years. A rough estimate of word count? Five million or more. But to find that right combination of words for this instant, this moment now upon me? Maybe I have to go back to Thorton Wilder's *Our Town*, when Emily asks, "Do people really know how incredible life truly is while they are still alive?"

Of all the moments of my life, this was such a moment.

Here I am sitting in a chair behind a table. My first glimpse of *her* is actually at waist level. She was wearing a well tailored gray pleated skirt, very tasteful calf-high leather boots, a black top, and leather jacket ... all of this in that first half second or so. I raised my glance ready to offer as I have for years, for thousands of fans, a friendly smile, a "Hi, thanks for coming..."

But I could not find the words to speak. At that precise instant her guardian angels did their magic, call it pixie dust, call it Spielberg quality special effects. Her left eye, a stunning green/gold color, actually sparkled. So help me, it was a flash of light ... and it was a lightning bolt straight into my heart.

I couldn't speak, I just stared into her eyes. She had the most remarkable smile which has captivated me ever since. Those eyes, that smile, wisps of reddish hair framing her face like a halo.

I just gazed at her, paralyzed.

She started to talk first. And I cannot recall a single word of what she said!

She would tell me later that she didn't even have a book to sign (more about that later). She just started to talk, something about an idea for marketing my book to film, or a series. I still can't remember what it was. I just should add here that I often have people come up and offer suggestions about how to market my books or turn them into movies, I smile politely and offer a thank you, but honestly it is rare that the suggestion is not something I haven't heard before or thought of myself.

But this time?

She started to talk and I think I must have looked like a deer in the headlights, perhaps slack-jawed as well. Her words? Honestly, I can laugh about it later, but it was just like in the old Charlie Brown cartoons when an adult spoke and it just came out as "wa-waaa-wa-wah-wawa-waaaa."

I couldn't comprehend a single word of what she was saying!

And I do need to make something clear here very clear. I'm a very normal, healthy guy. More than once in an autograph line, or hey, almost any given day since I turned fourteen, I'll see a woman and well … you know how it is … it's, "Wow she's hot!"

Ohhh yes, this woman before me was and always will be an 11 on a scale of 10. But this was all different from that. In fact it would take quite a few days before thoughts along those lines even began to emerge (really that's the truth)!

This might seem overdone or schmaltzy, but have you

ever seen a movie where an angel shows up? I mean a really "hot" angel? Maybe it's my Catholic upbringing but when a great-looking angel shows up in a movie it just doesn't seem right to observe "certain attributes" of hers! Maybe that isn't quite the right way to express those first seconds of reaction ... perhaps a better way is that I found myself looking past all of the exteriors (except for that magnetic gaze) to something deeper within.

I had met my twin flame.

She was still talking. I guess I was still nodding and smiling, maybe witnesses could tell me that I actually was trying to make some intelligent reply.

By this point several minutes must have passed. Some semblance of consciousness was returning. The line of people was still there, at least twenty or thirty more to go and, oh my gosh, they were not giving her the friendliest of smiles.

Meanwhile, overhead, the two guardian angel teams were mingling, watching, whispering in our ears. I think the head of my team was freaking on the special effects team of her side who had pulled off the eye sparkle. But it could still fall apart! I could just sit there like a gaping fish out of water until finally she just smiled and walked away.

No! Say something, do something! My guardian angels were screaming at me. Do something!

I finally blurted out something coherent even though I didn't understand a word she had said.

"Ahhh, that's really fascinating ... uhhh, could we continue this conversation later?"

I nodded to the restless crowd behind her.

"Ahhh ... would you mind waiting a few minutes while I sign books for the rest of these people?" (Actually I wanted every last one of them to flack off, disappear, teleport into a different dimension.) So help me, it was like some 1960s movie at that moment, the way the camera would focus on Audrey Hepburn or Julie Christie and everything else goes into soft focus.

She smiled and said something like, "Sure, I'll wait." And then? The editor of a paper for whom I would later find out she wrote an editorial column, asked if he could take a photograph of her with me. I motioned for her to come around the table and she knelt by my side.

Talk about a swoon moment! She leaned in, only inches away from me. I could catch the scent of her and it was overwhelming, my was heart racing.

Then she stood up again. I asked if she'd mind waiting? She nodded and smiled in reply and then slowly, very feminine, walked away.

What came next? That most deadly of female gestures: a turn of the head, a glance back over her left shoulder at me, again that eye contact. It is the universal gesture of "come hither" and, "Yeah I am interested in you." Read Conrad Lorenz and his observation of how birds first approach each other, the female first lowering her gaze but then turning to look back, a major class-one signal of interest.

At that moment I think the leader of my guardian angel team staggered, jaw dropping, cigar falling from his mouth. Her guardian angel was smiling knowingly at him with a "gotcha" look. The rest of the team on both sides were grinning, hers winking at mine, who stopped their high-fiving and just stood there with foolish grins in reply.

My angel team leader finally got his senses back together. "All right guys, it only took forty-plus years to get to this moment and more than a few mistakes. Now let's not screw this up. Be ready to push him." Then, looking over at her team, "And for heaven's sake keep her there! Don't let her leave!"

TWIN FLAME

Meanwhile, back down on earth ten feet below, there I was, staring at a line of very patient people, maybe a few had some sort of inkling of what had just happened, but the rest? They wanted books signed and wanted to talk.

I'll confess, the next ten minutes were a blur and perhaps I was more than a bit rude to those who had patiently waited, and if you who are reading this were on that line, my apologies to you and I think you now understand.

The next person came up, set book down to be signed, and clearly wanted to say something. I dashed off an autograph, "Thank you ... next please! Thank you ... next please! Thank you, gee I'm glad the book helped change your life ... next please!"

Half the time I was looking over to her ... and then a flash of anxiety. A guy I knew who had attended previous conferences had zeroed in on her, walked straight up to her and had started hitting on her. Competition! Of course that triggered the alpha male response.

It really got me going with the signings. I was nearly out of the chair ready to just walk down the waiting line, "Come on folks, hurry it up, let's get a move on here!"

And then after what seemed an eternity but was most likely not more than ten minutes, I signed the last book. Most of that time, I kept looking over at her. I swear that if she had started to walk away I'd have just said to heck with the rest of the line, gotten up and run after her. Already this overwhelming sense, this incredible rush, that the most important moment of my life was unfolding here in a conference center up in the mountains of North Carolina.

The book for the last person was signed and I stood up. I recall a couple of people heading towards the stage, wanting autographs or to chat and though I hated to be rude I acted like I didn't see them, left the table and walked the thirty feet or so to where she was waiting. There could have been a field of hot coals and I'd have gone over them not just barefoot, but on my hands and knees. I had to talk with her! I nervously approached, the competition obviously trying to make headway, but as I drew closer her eye contact shifted directly to me and did not waiver.

No one else was in that cavernous auditorium but her. It really was like those soft focus moments in a David Lean movie. I think I smiled, offered a thanks for her patience and suggested that we step outside to talk. The poor guy who was trying for her was left in the dust. Hey, when you've hit that moment in your life, it really is "All's fair…" There was no hesitation on her part. She smiled and walked by my side to the exit.

TWIN FLAME

Chapter One Narration:
The Opening of the Heart

> "It lies not in our power to love, or hate,
> For will in us is over-ruled by fate…
> Who ever loved, that loved not at first sight"
> - Christopher Marlowe

We prepare for love with open hearts, great expectations and the naiveté of young teens. The reality for most is hot sex, little emotion and lack of interest in commitment. One of the partners is more devoted and ultimately is severely wounded by the other during the inevitable break up. It is the wounded partner who almost immediately begins the quest to search for the "one." The ideal love of a lifetime emerges as a vision with desired characteristics. On some occasions they emerge in vivid dreams. The anticipated and visualized new partner might be blond and blue eyed and brilliant or he or she could be dark-skinned, assertive and entrepreneurial. Make no mistake, this is a searching process — a process that will ultimately make one feel whole.

The image of the soul-mate is perhaps imprinted before birth in the deoxyribonucleic acid. During the prepubescent attractions we begin the process of formulating preferences. Proper socialization ensures our attractions and subsequent pursuit. The experience of the first love affair is enlightening and terrifying at the same time. We yearn to become whole by finding our one true love but lack the methodology to proceed. It is said in Greek Mythology that Zeus split humans in half as punishment and they forever wandered trying to find their other half in a soul-mate.

The quest begins in earnest after the first break up with a prior significant other. Months and sometime years pass before the chance meeting of the love who will become the twin flame. In an utterly unexpected chance encounter people sometimes from opposite ends of the country meet and recognize a mysteriously mutual attraction. They finish each others' sentences, hold the same political views and both love sushi. Just looking at the other's face they feel as if they are home and at peace with life. All of the chakras are spinning in unison, or so it seems. It is an intimate dance complete with passion beyond the wild dreams of either of them. The vibrational pull toward a partnership at this point is as intense as anything that ever motivated them to act on impulse.

So what is really happening here in the first chapter, "In The Beginning?" Grant is reminiscing about November 2nd, 2013, as the most important day of his life because it was on that day he met his potentially future soul-mate, Charlotte. It clearly had the probability of being the most important day of his life, but there was no way of knowing that at the time. Perhaps the saints, poets and bodhisattva's, the more enlightened beings, knew in advance how this would play out. They of course stay in the present moment in a mindfulness not experienced by most people. They do not ponder the future or constantly dwell on the negatives of the past which preclude experiencing that present moment of attentiveness.

There were many paths toward or against this twin flame relationship — would it burn out or perhaps be the start of a lifetime of love? The paths might take them to ecstatic joy or horrific sorrow, or both, during their karmic phase. All the other relationships they had ever experienced would play a key role in the outcome. Karma is a word that is frequently misconstrued. If Karma is defined as the sum of a person's actions from the past it is missing a few major points. It is a more complex concept. The seeds are planted by our bad and good actions as we think, speak and actively commit deeds of compassion, love or rage and anger. The concept of Karma acts as an intellectual catalyst to grow and become kinder and more tolerant in each subsequent relationship.

Mental chatter is inescapable after a break up and if change is going to happen, this is the time it has the best potential. Change that will permit the start of a twin flame process. All of the prior relationship fighting, the break ups, the divorces and the mental disquietude catapults the individual to maturity and self actualization so that when the moment arises they are prepared for the twin flame process, or so they think.

Jung teaches us on the synchronicity of karma: "When an inner situation is not made conscious, it appears outside as fate."

The perfection of a potential relationship meeting at this point includes all of the lessons learned and nostalgia of the high points of prior partnering. The mental flashbacks include the passion of the love making and the agony of the fighting. The financial disasters of the divorces, the child custody fights and the single parenting.

By far the worst memories are from the tangential friends and relatives who inevitably take sides at the end or even during the prior marriages. The so-called "best buddies" who move in to console the wounded partner and offer advice on how to retaliate and find revenge. Hollywood is always producing a new movie with an ex dropping a package on fire at the front door of the ex loaded with dog poop. The audience laughs and the Karma takes a downward spiral.

Yes, revenge, retaliation and reconstruction are the three usual aspects of the end of a relationship. Obviously not taking the Karmic lessons seriously, this is a fact of life and happens frequently. If that isn't bad enough, both exes must endure the spiritual advisers, who present themselves as the alternative to the big bad dude the person just broke up with. The spiritual advisers are full of controlling plans and methodology on how to properly manage another human's life. The cycle continues, bad marriage, bad dating, delay of the bliss that a soul-mate brings. The reality is a delay of game in ever finding a soul-mate while under the control of narcissistic advisers who always, it seems, have their own agenda. The future twin soul partnership can be delayed for years by these friends, family and advisers. There is a singular path to opening to a twin flame relationship and that is the self actualized realization of relying on no one but yourself to move forward.

Chapter Two

~
I'd Like to Get to Know You...

Walking out the side door of the auditorium with *her* by my side, my heart was racing. I would learn that her name was Charlotte.

Memory is such a fascinating thing. Little do we realize how much our mind is actually processing and storing every single second. It is said that we have five senses, and that each of us use them in different ways and in various orders of priority. Some of us are more visual, others more auditory and so on.

There are moments in our lives that are so incredibly intense that time actually does seem to slow down and we focus on remarkable details, while all the time our brain is racing to process it all and shift it into conscious thought.

The fifty feet or so to that side exit? Ask me to recall anything, anyone beyond Charlotte, and memory is a blank. Within me all attention was focused on her. The way her eyes glanced up to meet mine. That alone is a fascinating aspect of who we are, how we all interact. Ever have anyone look into your eyes and you actually feel a chill of warning that sets your defensive instincts on edge? To look straight into someone's eyes, especially someone who you think is a stranger, can be intimidating. I should add here that I am considered extremely tall at nearly six feet, five inches, while Charlotte is a petite five foot, six. Later on she would admit that at times my physical size relative to her is intimidating. But at that moment, it was near constant eye contact and smiles as I approached.

In those first exchanged glances what were we saying without a word being spoken? Indeed volumes upon volumes of feelings. "I trust you" was a big one. "You intrigue me." "Who are you, really?" "What is happening here between us?" and yes, even some fear. Whether you are sixteen or sixty, the dating scene, those first moments of meeting someone and that instant wondering, "Can this be someone special in my life?" can definitely be anxiety-provoking. Will the glances trigger something and one or both of us "put up our shields?"

There was the visual for me, that smile, the way her hair was so neatly arranged, her makeup just enough but not too much or none at all … what a clue there that this was a person who took pride in her appearance but not to overwhelm.

All of this in the few seconds it took to reach the door and step outside.

Where to stand? Not too close, that would be intimidating, but not too far apart. There were others around us of course, folks were still leaving the auditorium for a break, some approaching, wanting to talk to me, and frankly I just gave off signals that my attention now was for this one person only.

I was nervous. This could end a minute from now, one wrong or misread signal which terminates with a polite smile, a hand shake, a "nice to meet you," and then a walking away.

I knew something stunningly remarkable was beginning to unfold, but did she? I did know this for certain. If she turned and walked away now she would haunt me.

I'm a fan of old movies. There is a scene in *Citizen Kane* where an elderly gentleman is being interviewed, mention is made of memories of the past, of regrets and longings. The old man smiles wistfully and recalls a day when he was taking the ferry across the Hudson River to

New York. And there he saw a young woman. He sighed at the mention of her and then went on to say that across fifty years not a day goes by that he does not think of her.

Would that be my fate? It must have been registering somewhere in my subconscious. Would this be a moment that might pass away like a spring time dew that evaporates into a misty dream and would linger on for years of regret and longing?

I know now as I write this that such thoughts were forming for her as well, but back then, at just after noon of November 2, 2013, I did not yet know what was happening within her. I do now as I write this and smile.

She made the opening move of conversation. Recall that she had joined the autograph line without a book, with a quickly made up suggestion about seeing additional works covering different points of view of what I write about. Frankly, I had heard such before, but coming from her, every word was suddenly golden and I responded politely, thanking her for what she had to say.

And then she shifted the topic, such a beautiful move, be it from within her or guided by our guardian angels.

She commented how during my talk I mentioned my daughter several times and asked about her. What a bonding moment that was. Obviously, both Charlotte and I had been married before, both of us had gone through tragic difficult experiences, and both of us had one child, daughters of similar age. What parent does not want to talk about her child?

I told her a bit about mine, a pre-med student at Chapel Hill, made the polite but genuine gesture back of asking her if she had children and she lit up. A key bit of information there! When young and dating how often did our elders offer the sage advice to take a look at the entire family before getting too far in? We all have dysfunctional families in one way or another. But there is dysfunction and then there is real dysfunction, that should be a warning sign! Dating when older? Take a long look at the relationship between parent and child. The way they first speak of their kids is important. When older of course you have to assume there is a divorce in the past (if they are being honest with you)! How is the relationship with the kids now? Is there closeness? Even if not the primary care giver, is there that pride and familiarity? Or a distance? Or even abandonment, which was always a signal for me to turn and head the other way. Charlotte happily opened up about her daughter, speaking proudly of how she had just started her first year at Carnegie Mellon, majoring in mechanical engineering, and then she threw a curve ball straight at me.

"My daughter has Asperser's Syndrome."

Wow, what a revealing statement in those first five minutes. She was looking straight into my eyes as she said that, and would later admit it was a test. You raise a child with Asperser's and it becomes the focus of your life. The test? Would I blink, mutter inwardly, "Whoa, time to leave," or just stand there with an ignorant blank stare and reply, "What's that?"

I've been a teacher for nearly forty years, at the start working at a boarding school that specialized in learning disabilities. An "Aspie?" I have always seen them as a unique gift to our world. They can be a challenge that can drive those who love them to distraction, but, like a diamond, they might be the hardest of stones to work with, but if you help to shape them, how stunning the results! The term Asperger's did not begin to emerge until some time in the late 1970s. Prior to that, those displaying such outward signs were lumped in with the definition of autism, and not too far further back autistics were simply defined as "retarded." How tragic.

At the boarding school I first worked at in the 1970s I was a dorm parent for over fifty students, many who were defined at that time as dyslexic. In fact it was while first working there that the headmaster, a beloved mentor to not just students but to faculty as well, arranged for me to be evaluated by a specialist under the guise that I was visiting that specialist to discuss a student with whom we were having serious problems. When that specialist, after a couple of hours of friendly conversation, focused in on me (without my realizing what he was actually doing, was testing me during our conversation), he compassionately told me that I was severely dyslexic.

The scales truly did fall away from my eyes as he pronounced that diagnosis, and frankly I just sat there and cried. Why was it that a few certain things with learning and interacting with others came so easily, while others were impossible to grasp and more than one teacher had treated me with contempt, declaring that I was lazy and even stupid? It was hell. Some testing when I was six showed that I had what used to be called a genius I.Q., but then only a few years later my parents were being told that I was mentally disabled and needed to be held back and put into special education.

There I was in 1978, my first teaching job at a school specializing in learning disabilities, who the headmaster had hired less than a half hour into our interview, after years of barely squeezing through college and six long years after graduation of not being able to find a teaching job. Years of my loving parents being driven to distraction over my academic failure and yet paradoxically being told when I was six that my I.Q. was darn near off the charts. I believe that I flunked foreign languages at least five or six times from junior high through college. My spelling was at a fifth grade level and physically I could not even write a readable sentence on a piece of paper. I could not even stay between the lines and often would shred the paper in the process.

Thanks to that beloved headmaster, his "reading" me in the interview, and sending me to that specialist changed my life. There is even a guardian angel story tied into that moment, but I'll save that for another time. Why did he hire me? After meeting with the specialist in Boston I had a long drive back to the school where I had just been hired. I did a lot of thinking during that three-hour drive about who I was, why did I think the way I did, and what did this diagnosis mean about me? I sought out my new boss who had arranged for my testing, sat down with him and, yeah, I started to cry again. The revelation that I was severely dyslexic had come as one hell of a shock, but also a relief. That brilliant headmaster and master teacher had put my life into such a positive perspective, telling me that he hired me because he knew that with my "talents" (not disabilities, instead it was talents), I would better understand my students and reach them in ways that other teachers could not. He told me to embrace what I was because I had a unique gift, not a disability, and learn to make the most of it.

And thus it was so. In fact, during that incredible time working with that headmaster, I was not just teaching history, I was learning from my kids about the way they thought, the way they struggled and coped, and learned as well.

What I learned helped me to develop what the psychologists might call "coping skills." I'll call it rewiring synapses within my brain around those areas that, by the definition of others, were short-circuited and how to work around it. That learning process would enable me later to go on to a top-level graduate school for a Ph.D. in history, eventually teach at a college level, and yes, become a professional author as well with a number of best-selling books.

So as I listened to Charlotte drop that first bit of personal, intimate detail into our opening conversation, "My daughter has Asperger's." It touched deep into my heart.

I could see the look in her eyes, a flash of warning that if the conversation was to continue on the trajectory towards twin flames there should be recognition and understanding.

It therefore came from the heart what I said in reply:

"I see Asperger's as genius by a different definition."

The look in her eyes at my response touched my heart. It was like we had exchanged some sort of secret code for a mystical society and knew that the other understood all that it meant.

And thus did the conversation now flow. You might know what I mean, that both of you are so excited you just want to pour everything out as quickly as possible … like watching two children, old buddies, from summer camp a year earlier who, when reunited, hurriedly tell the other all the latest news before running off to play together.

I think about twenty or so minutes passed. And yes, I smoked a few cigarettes. Charlotte did not say a word but I sensed that I had just chalked up a negative point. She let it go without comment. (Less than a week later I flushed the remnants of a pack down the toilet and quit cold turkey, though I would pull some old pipes out of a closet which did pass muster with her!)

We drifted back inside, the auditorium all but empty, and sat down side by side to talk.

I was enthralled, but a few tough questions lingered:

married or not? Age? Was there someone else in the picture at the moment?

Married? She knew I wasn't, I had already made reference to raising my daughter on my own. There was no ring on her finger, but still? So I rather woodenly asked how her husband had reacted to the Asperger's diagnosis. A shake of the head, a bit of a sad laugh, "Oh we divorced years ago."

I sighed with relief. We were through the first gate but a long way from being fully cleared to move forward. Next: age? This was going to be tough. I knew there was a major age difference. Okay, I had just turned 63. Just writing out my age is still a shocker. I mean what the heck is going on with this time thing? Wasn't I just twenty-five a day ago? I still feel like I'm no more than forty. I'm blessed with great genes from both sides of my family, but still … inwardly that age thing freaks me. Does it really go this quickly?

Charlotte? So incredibly youthful and beautiful, sitting next to me, eyes sparkling, an energy radiating. Good Lord in heaven please don't let her be thirty-five, which is where I guessed her to be. Ten years age difference, okay. Twenty gets a bit weird. Thirty, I had to realistically accept that it would just be impossible. Far too many issues and simply the biggest of all, how could I ever ask someone to be with me, when statistically it could very well mean so many years apart later?

I asked to see a picture of her daughter, having produced one of mine. She opened her wallet, driver's license clearly visible, and I tried to catch the birthdate! It was really awkward and way too obvious, the same as asking her about her husband. I couldn't see it clearly enough to read. It was obvious what I was doing and I lamely just blurted out the question, "How old are you?"

Awkward indeed! She smiled, said she was forty-one, about to turn forty two.

Hmm ... just over twenty-one years, a bit much. More on that issue later but for the moment it was not a deal killer if she was still sitting there and it had to be obvious to her by now just how interested I was in her.

Were there other guys in the picture? It was way too awkward to try for that big question. In our brief time together so far I already could tell she was an honest soul. In fact by this point if there was someone else in her life she would have already given me a wave-off signal, the type of comment politely given such as, "I wish my boyfriend were here to meet you, he'd be delighted." Shut down but done so politely and allowing a graceful retreat.

I figured to definitely let that question of another in her life pass for the moment. Another moment when I smile as I am writing this. A guy might not be able to pick up the more subtle signals of, "Is there someone else?" but girls really have an advantage when it comes to that one.

She would later comment that my entire appearance shouted, "No woman in my life!" I was never one to comb my hair, for starters. I have very fine hair (and fortunately at my age still a full head covering of it!) so however it dried after a shower, that's the way it sat. No woman who really cared would let me out the door like that, especially to give a speech. Also I was in serious need of a trim. My clothes, which for me was formal wear, included a jacket. (At my height it is hard to find clothing that really fits well, again a department a caring woman would see to. It would be Charlotte who would introduce me to a fascinating fact: I can actually buy clothes and have them tailored to fit.) And then the dog hair. At that time one of my beloved golden retrievers was still alive, and evidence of her was all over my jacket and pants. So she was already getting the vibe that there was no one serious in my life.

The next half hour or so of talk went by in a blur and then I noticed there were some people hanging about a polite distance away but obviously wanting to talk to me. Dang, it was time to "meet and greet" again, something I am terrible at. The organizers of the conference had set up a tent pavilion outside the auditorium where folks could get something to eat. I knew that once we stepped out the door, I would get swamped. Normally I'm okay with that, but today? I wanted to hang on to the conversation with Charlotte as long as possible and she was not giving off any signals like, "It was nice chatting with you but I have to go home now and wash my hair," or something like that.

I made some mention that I had to go outside, we stood up, and then those delightful guardian angels came back into the game. The conference center is located on a lake and on the far shore I could see a darkness sweeping towards us. Though early in November it looked just like a rain wall of an approaching thunderstorm ... and it was coming on fast!

Talk about a Divine Intervention, this one was it! Not thirty seconds later, as we were lingering at the door to go outside to eat the catered lunch, a mighty wind hit and upended a side of the tent pavilion that was covering the food, sending the crowd scattering. I think I actually did laugh at that moment! I looked over at Charlotte and she was grinning as well.

She glanced at the askew tent and said, "That's a shame," and then pulled out her phone. "Let me find a place for lunch."

It turned out that the conference center had a dining room across the road that the vast majority of folks attending the conference did not know about and, even as the storm passed as swiftly as it had miraculously arrived, we made a dash for it.

What unfolded then were two more hours of sitting and talking and now, two and a half years later, it is hard to recall all that was said. It really was like two old friends from long ago reconnecting, both all so eager to pour out their thoughts to the other and eager as well to soak up every word said in reply.

It finally came time for Charlotte to head for home, no comments about a date waiting for her that evening, nor from me an offer of one, everything was still in such a whirl within me.

As we walked to the parking lot there was one final coup arranged for me that day. I had just received an advance copy of my latest novel; it was still in the car and I planned to give it to my friend who had organized the conference. Needless to say, my friend was not going to get that copy.

I slowed by my car, told Charlotte that I'd like to give her a book and as I went to unlock it there was a loud exclamation, "*That's* your car?!"

I couldn't help but inwardly grin with that one. You see, I own a Nissan 350Z ... red, of course.

For a hundred years cars have been marketed to guys with a barely concealed aspect of sexuality to them. It's funny to look at an old magazine from say, the sixties or seventies when it was a lot more overt. Hot sports car equals sexy girl: HSC=SG. Throughout my teens and twenties I was a confirmed Volkswagen bug guy. Why? That was all I could afford. For my generation it had a certain counter-culture appeal, but definitely was not sexy. A buddy of mine in college owned a Datsun 280Z and it seemed like there was always an incredible girl by his side as he went roaring off campus.

Not to say that that is why I finally brought a 350Z as a post-divorce car in my mid-fifties. The truth, and I mean the real truth, is that after my separation, having given the primary car to my soon-to-be ex, I went out shopping for a vehicle. I checked out BMWs and Audis, which I actually came close to buying but the annoying sales agent wouldn't budge on negotiating and kept trying to pressure for a sale.

On a Friday afternoon, eight years before meeting Charlotte, I picked my daughter up from school and we went out car hunting together. We went back to the Audi place one more time, the sales person was still a jerk, and my daughter whispered, "Let's get out of here, and besides I don't like the car."

We were driving past the Nissan dealership, which had used vehicles on an adjoining lot and my daughter shouted out, "There's your car, Dad!" and pointed at that lovely Z.

We stopped and if there can be a bit of a "twin flame" between a man and something mechanical, it sure hit that day as well ... the same way it hit me the first time I saw my 1943 Aeronca L3-B "warbird" airplane.

The VIN number and price were on the side windshield, my daughter copied it down, and we got out of there before the ubiquitous salesman came rushing over.

I did the homework, called up a friend who knows cars, got the straight info on the model I was looking at, and the following morning, taking a cue from the old Bill Crosby show, I dressed down to old jeans and a slightly smelly t-shirt and went back to try the car out.

Six hours later I was driving it home. Yeah, I do have a thing for fast cars and antique airplanes; perhaps it's an overcompensation for my nerd factor.

Eight years later in that conference center parking lot,

it finally paid off big time. Charlotte was, and still is, a hot car nut. I could see her just staring at my Z with scarcely concealed desire to try it out. The only insult to that moment? Later on she would admit that, with my being a college professor and author, she had assumed that I'd be a Volvo or Saab kind of guy. Ugh!

So I handed her the book, autographed it, and pointedly added my email address below my signature. There was a lingering final glance as I walked her over to her car, a bit of a stodgy SUV, and watched her pull out of the parking lot.

Yeah, I was a bit of an idiot. I didn't have her phone number or email address. The ball was absolutely in her court if the conversation was to continue. But then again, I would learn later it played in my favor. Charlotte is indeed an absolutely stunning woman and regularly had to shun off guys a bit too eager to go out with her. I figured my deferring on asking that traditional question about a phone call or a date might just win a point ... which it did. Thank you, guardian angels for that bit of guidance that I suspect was conveyed over by her own guardian angels.

The drive home was memorable. The radio was on; I think it was the only time in my life I actually had a football game on the radio while driving. The regular talk show program was preempted. But I hardly heard it.

Okay this is going to sound really nerdy but an old song came to me and I just couldn't shake it. A song from the late sixties, "I'd Like to Get to Know You."

Look up the words sometime. Unlike the tone of so many love songs, or today's "lust songs," this one has a beautiful statement in it: that no promise can be made yet, but "I sure would like to get to know you."

I finally got home and I actually ran into the house. My daughter was home from college that weekend; she barely got a hello from me. I raced to my computer which is always on, clicked on my email and exclaimed, "Oh my God, She Wrote to Me!"

Chapter Two Narration:
Initial Encounter

The initial attraction is charged with all of the attributes of the most profound infatuation in life, the in love-at-first-sight moment. It seems unusual for Grant and Charlotte to meet during a book signing, but in reality most soul-mates find each other in unusual places. The unexpected places are where it frequently happens. A glimpse of the perfect person emerges in your peripheral vision as she walks into your office just as you prepare to close your briefcase at the end of a very long day. Your eyes meet and it feels like a slow motion movie running toward a lover in a field of lavender. The instant your eyes meet you feel the electrical pulse known only to twin flames. It resonates with both people and their fate is sealed.

In ancient times when historical Buddha walked the earth, the culture had this first meeting down to a science. They checked out the potential mate with a mental list of thirty-two attributes. In one quick look the potential partner entering the room was rated on everything from intellect to appearance. If the charge attraction was there, they had more information about potential compatibility! In America courtship was historically a process where the male pursued the female to learn more about each other with the specific intentional outcome being marriage. The female who participate equally can indicate receptiveness or rejection as can the male.

In modern times we are so much more romantic, so sure that our visual attractions and subsequent dating practices will bring us the same high-pitched face vibrational joy as we had the moment we met. We push the thoughts from our minds in the beginning that we may be coming from different religions, age gaps and sometimes even lack of compatibility. The way a person handles stress can create monumental problems down the road in the relationship.

Caution is not permitted, but rather the adventuresome persona pushes the go-for-it plan of action. There is no turning back to think, reflect or seek counsel on the relationship. It's happening and nothing will stand in the way. Dating is initiated by either the male or female in modern America and has no plan, intention or direction other than fun and getting to know the other person. The process is initially pleasant but can create the type of anxiety experienced in the early moments of this relationship when both had anxiety speculating on the likelihood that the other is interested. The signals and answers eventually emerged and Grant and Charlotte began the dance.

In this phase the soul-mate is sheer perfection. When "he" enters a room the smile on her face is radiant. When "she" leans forward to change the channel "he" offers to assist. Car doors are opened, formal dinner parties are planned using the Bavarian china and Francis the First sterling silver flatware. This is it: the perfect relationship. The Saturday date night is complete with French wine and pheasant under glass. There are tickets for the latest off-Broadway play. The effort to maintain the mundane tasks involving the job or homework are placed in a secondary position to the "relationship." The life of the soul-mate is almost existing in a utopian plane oblivious to the world around. The sheer perfection of coming together "in relationship" is all that matters.

The twin flames are madly in love and the rest of the world is of little importance. "She" used to watch tennis tournaments during her first marriage. Now, she watches her partner take a nap, she enjoys the way he eats, fills the bird feeder, tosses a ball to his dogs. "He" used to watch TV news, never missing the primetime analysis of the daily events. Now, he watches her prepare a bubble bath, apply her make up and especially enjoys watching her shave her legs. He finds great joy in watching her weed and water the garden and fertilize her flowers. They only see each other and are only happy when they are entwined together.

Entwined together ... there is a small spider less than a centimeter found in Australia called the peacock. The male peacock spider dances for love by chasing the female with a series of abdominal thrusts and producing an ornately colorful fan off his tail. He moves his appendages in what looks like a dance of perhaps a creative traffic cop's arm movement in intense traffic to offer direction to drivers. Several males dance for one female simultaneously and when they sense she lacks interest and obviously rejects them, they flee quickly to avoid being her lunch! The one lucky male who is accepted by the female is not much better off because after the mating she devours him anyway. Human dating is a dance, ritualistic by cultural norms and loaded with rejection, insecurity and yes, peacock strutting. It either produces moving into relationship and joy, or abandonment and rejection. Thankfully, the human dating rituals don't end in a New Jersey trip to the meadowlands.

TWIN FLAME

Chapter Three

Let the Courtship Begin!

Three days later:

Long emails followed within hours of our meeting, Charlotte broke what is supposed to be the old tradition that girls wait until the guy makes contact. Nope! I got home and a note was already there from her. I had let the ball bounce into her court when we said good bye in the conference center parking lot. I did not ask for her phone number, or even her email address, but I had given her mine. I was leaving the courtship decisions up to her … and why not?

A day later we were on the phone for a couple of hours that just seemed to float by in a few minutes. And then such a wonderful opening synchronicity came into play. Months before we met, Charlotte had acquired five acres of land from her parents and was in the process of starting construction on a house. More on that later, for the house was definitely a metaphor for who she is and what she desires in life. But to the narrative of the moment: her new home would only be three miles from mine, just on the other side of the county line and she had to go to the county courthouse to take care of some permits. Guardian angels were definitely in high gear now … the airport where I hanger my two antique planes is just a couple of miles away from the courthouse. So of course the offer was obvious and of course I "already had plans" to go flying on the day that she would be going to the courthouse.

So thus it was that, three days after we met, I pulled into the courthouse parking lot at ten in the morning, after having spent the previous two hours at the airport prepping my plane so it would be ready to go.

Just seeing her standing there in the parking lot caused my heart to thump over while driving the few minutes to the airport. Charlotte followed me in her car. Would that overwhelming rush experienced when we met suddenly evaporate with this, our second meeting? Or, even worse, was all of this an illusion and would she politely but firmly make it clear within the next few hours that it was nice to have me as "just a friend?" How those three words can be so dreadful ... just a friend!

Fascinating, the backwards and forwards dance of courtship, the opening steps of utter fascination combined with the inner fears: is she just being polite, will something either of us say or do shatter the illusion and a colder reality hits, the age thing that is out there and I knew it ... would that be a veto for her?

So this was one very nervous suitor (and pilot) who pulled up to my hanger,. As she got out of her car I was greeted with that stunningly warm smile, and again the sparkle in her eyes.

A side point here about me and flying. I've had a fascination with flying ever since childhood. Because of my eyes I could not qualify for the Air Force, but nevertheless, while still in college, I started flight lessons on my own for a private license, saving up enough from my $2.50 an hour job to pay the twenty dollars for an hour-long lesson. And those of you who are pilots can figure out how long ago that was when you could fly with an instructor for twenty dollars an hour!

Flying eventually went by the wayside in my mid-twenties because I simply could not afford it, especially when I took my first job as a teacher. The years passed and eyes turning enviously to the sky whenever someone flew over on "laughter silvered wings." Decades passed and, at last, ten years back I returned to the air. Going through a tough divorce, friends counseled me to pick up a hobby for diversion. A very wise friend, a pilot who would die in a tragic crash, repeatedly said that my soul should be up in the sky and I could easily get a sports pilot license.

So thus it was that one day I wandered into a small grass strip airport to just look around, and, thirty minutes later, I was totally in love. when the head mechanic at the airport, a man who would become one of my closest friends, showed me an original 1943 World War II reconnaissance plane that was up for sale. Before the day was out I had put down a deposit on it.

Impulsive? Heck yeah! It would mean learning to fly all over again, in an airplane that handled quite differently from what I had first learned in. An antique plane, older than I am, is a precious historic heirloom and the responsibility of flying her safely touched me deeply. Also, it is definitely old-fashioned, stick and rudder with a bit of a "seat-of-the-pants" thrown in to learn how to fly an antique "tail dragger" airplane. My first lesson left me drenched with nervous sweat, and wondering if I was indeed more than a little crazy. But then? As my favorite poem states, I was again dancing on "laughter silvered wings," where, pointed heavenward, one can indeed "reach out to touch the face of God." For some of us who are truly lucky, flying becomes something spiritual. Check out what Richard Bach writes; he can explain what those moments are like far better than I can.

That was back seven years or more before the day I met Charlotte and flying had indeed become the passion of my life. She would later joke that from the moment she saw me with that plane she knew who my mistress was, and she was okay with it.

It was a major win point for her right there. More than

a few of you most likely know of a relationship with a partner who might tacitly accept such an interest when first dating but later on? "You're spending money on that again?" Hey, if someone cannot understand such a passion and accept it, perhaps even eventually embrace it, is she really your twin flame? The fact that Charlotte understood from the moment she first saw me with my beloved L3 was a huge win for both of us.

But it was not the plane we would fly that day. I had a second plane in partnership with a friend, an antique as well, with a bit more of a stable platform, especially for a first flight with someone, so that was the plane I had rolled out.

Together we went through the pre-flight check, my explaining how everything worked and why, helped her get in, did a final safety review with her, and then those two words I so love to hear and say, "Clear prop!"

The engine roared to life, we taxied out, I carefully reviewed things with her one more time, and finally the moment of rolling out on to the runway arrived. I always say a brief prayer before taking off, did so, looked over at her and her features were lit with an approving smile. We had not yet talked seriously about issues of faith and our relationships with God, but that prayer, part of my personal "pre-flight check list" was important to me.

I throttled up, the plane lurched forward. There were tense seconds that every pilot feels as you're giving quick glances to your gauges, picking up the feel of your bird with your hand on the stick, feet subtly dancing on the rudder pedals, scanning ahead. There is a lot to do in those first fifteen seconds. And then that incredible rush as you lift off the ground, vibration from the wheels ceasing, speed picking up, end of the runway dropping down below you … all of your instruments are showing good, then finally that first turn.

I sent a sidelong glance to her and, oh my gosh, she was grinning with delight! If nervous, she wasn't showing it; she was absolutely absorbed in the moment, the joy of flying. I know her guardian angels were looking over at mine (one of my guardian angels is a pilot) and grins of approval were exchanged. This woman likes flying, wow!

We flew to a nearby airport for a quick landing, a cup of coffee, then back up again. Charlotte paid the ultimate compliment to a pilot, "That was a great landing!"

There are several types of pilots out there, a classic definition being that, "There are old pilots, and then there are bold pilots, but there are very few old, bold pilots." There are also the type of pilots who are immature show-offs hitting a new passenger with the line, "Want to see what this baby can do?" and then proceed to scare the crap out of someone. Not this pilot. Every moment along the way I kept explaining what we were doing, asked what she wanted to see and even offered her the controls (of course I kept a light hold on them at the same time)!

An hour later we were back and rolled up to the hanger, with Charlotte helping me tuck the plane in and close things up. And then I made my bold move. She was excited about the flight and grinning with pleasure. I just couldn't help it or contain it a moment longer. Throughout the flight in that narrow cockpit we had been pressed side by side and, good heavens, I was so absolutely aware of her being that close but at the same time had to stay focused on flying safely.

We were back on the ground, our feet on terra firma, Charlotte just a foot away, guardian angels nudging me closer.

"Charlotte, can I kiss you?"

I just blurted it out. She looked up at me wide-eyed. A

pause, a nervous nod and I kissed Charlotte for the first time. It was brief, just a second or two, and absolutely electric. She would later say that up to that instant she wasn't really sure of my intentions but now it was clear.

A bit of a nervous withdraw, with my finally breaking the tension with the suggestion of lunch. Another major Rubicon with that. If the kiss had taken me into the wrong direction, here was the moment where she could have politely withdrawn, claimed a prior engagement of some sort and fled, to later that day send the "Let's just be friends" email. Instead I got a warm smile.

That lunch went for four hours! Tuesday is the day of the week when I teach full time in the afternoon and evening. After two hours sharing lunch I should have been on the road but just did not want the conversation to end. So, a confession to my college where I teach. There are priorities in life and at that moment there was one and only one priority. So I made my voice sound husky, called in to the dean's office, coughing and hacking, and a moment later looked back at her with a smile. We had two more hours to talk!

It was finally time to head back when our lunch date came to an end. I walked her to her car and, emboldened, I asked permission for a second kiss. This one was a bit longer but I could now sense a bit of tension. She stepped back, made firm eye contact, and then dropped it on me.

"Grant, I have to be honest, I am talking to a couple of other guys."

Now was this the shut down? But then no follow up that she was getting serious with one. Just that she was "talking to" some other guys. What the heck, it would be weird if she wasn't. I'll confess I inwardly smiled. In fact I admired her response … this woman was dead-on honest. If anything it was a bit of a challenge.

Early winter twilight was settling in as I raced to campus to barely make my evening class in time. I recall it as a difficult class for me to stay focused on. My mind was brimming with but one thought.

The drive home, another mad race. I knew it would be one of two things and, you know what I feared, a polite thank you for the day and those dreaded three words, "Just be friends."

It is fascinating to now compare notes with Charlotte long afterwards. What she was thinking as she drove home. The two kisses had made my intentions extremely clear. The one thing I feared, the age difference, she would later say she was seriously contemplating. But it was not a shut down. The dance would continue and she immediately composed a warm thank you email and yes ... left the door open for more!

How fascinating was this twin flames dance in its opening moves. That strange, giddy, near childlike delight, fantasies running wild, mingled with fear, anxiety, self doubts, wondering who the other really is.

It was definitely strategy time when I relaxed after reading her email and knew I was still in the running! Other guys were on the scene. Chances were, I figured, she most likely already had a date for Friday or Saturday night. Later I would know that wasn't the case, the "other two guys" was her just being honest that they were circling around but no date had materialized yet.

Time to be a bit preemptive, I figured. Go for a date mid-week, which would make my interest abundantly clear. I got on the phone and a half hour later the date was set for twenty-hours hence!

The First Dinner Date

Nineteen and a half hours later I was parked at a convenience store a quarter mile from her house. No, I wasn't doing anything creepy, like spying. I just wanted to get to her place exactly five minutes early and traffic around town could jam up at times. Better to take the time to be early rather than, no matter what the reason, late for that first formal date. The twenty-two minute wait seemed like forever. Anxiety again. Was I fooling myself? Would something unravel? Here I am in my early sixties feeling a head-over-heels eighteen-year-old infatuation. Thoughts of Frank Sinatra songs like, "The Tender Trap" and "Witchcraft" played in my head. Was this some sort of witchcraft, or, "You're hooked, you're cooked, you're in the 'Tender trap?'"

Oh, what the heck, I'm caught, I realized, and damn glad that I am.

Exactly five minutes ahead of schedule I was at her door. Why five minutes? To show that I was prompt, reliable, and dying to see her again.

So off we go on our first dinner date which I had asked her to arrange. She made a perfect choice: a nice restaurant, not pricey, not cheap, just right in the middle. It was a subtle message by her saying, "I know you're a successful author and all that, but I am not interested in taking advantage of you." That was big for me. Later I'll tell some of the "nightmares from the cyber-meet-date world:" tales of the three-hundred dollar dinner, three cocktails before the meal is even done, and the woman is slurring and talking too loud, etc.

Charlotte had arranged everything perfectly, with understated elegance which so definitely connected. There was even a friendly but firm argument at the end of the meal when she tried to insist upon covering half the cost.

Good heavens, it was the first time that had ever happened to me on a date but my "old school" beliefs won out. A gentleman pays for dinner, end of discussion and no thank you, no feminist counter-arguments accepted. The fact that I could out-psych her with "rock-paper-scissors" and win 90% of the time sealed the argument the first night.

And then she hit the ball out of the park. For an after-dinner drink and dessert she suggested what was actually a favorite place, a wonderful old used book store where you could buy a glass of wine or champagne, wander around delightful, slightly musty book stacks that were interspersed with comfy sofas and old chairs, no music blaring, and just sit back and talk. That was another thing I hated about the dating scene, the loud restaurant or bar. So much of getting to know a person, at least for me, is about talking. Talking, not shouting, and she had found the perfect place for just that. We sat, of course, next to the history section.

Two hours of just talking ensued. Such two delightful hours, so relaxing that I suspect our guardian angels felt that all was well in hand, the twin flames were burning brighter. I mean I'm an author, a professor, a historian, old books stores are a perfect place to truly relax and let warm conversation flow.

And then, out of the blue, she knocked me over. It turned out we were both nerds, I mean real nerds! The topics drifted, each subject drawing us closer. We were starting to fill in the ends of each other's sentences or leap a split second ahead of the other to the next topic. Sooner or later it was bound to happen.

Star Trek.

I hope some of you reading this are not rolling your eyes, but I bet some of you are thinking, "Oh yeah." We discovered that both of us are rabid fans of the original series, and it was certainly a few extra points for me when I casually let it drop that I had written a Star Trek novel (even though it was for Next Generation).

Then she made her move. Smiling, she fell silent, eyes locked on mine, which of course turned my insides to jelly, and raised her hand, pointing fore and middle fingers heavenward.

A moment of silence.

"Know what this is?" she whispered, and, good Lord, her voice was a bit husky.

My mind was racing, what is it, *what is it*?

"Pon farr," she whispered.

Ohhhh My Gosh ... Pon farr, the Vulcan Mating Ritual!!!!

If you are a fan you already get it. Deep bass electric guitar notes, sliding down a scale, Mr. Spock breathing hard, looking more than a little crazed, the once-in-every-seven-years initiating move of the Vulcan mating ritual.

I was actually shaking as I raised my hand to meet hers, two fingers extended, intertwining them with hers, our eyes locked, both of us totally enwrapped with the other.

My God, we were having Vulcan foreplay right there in public!

The twin flames dance was definitely on.

Two Days Later

No, I am not skipping over something like a 1940s movie where Bogart kisses Bacall, the music swells, the scene dissolves, and in the next scene they are nestled together and sharing a cigarette. Far from it, actually. Our night out ended with my handing her the keys to my car. I knew she wanted to drive it; the hints were more than obvious. That night simply ended with a few more kisses, definitely more relaxed and warm. I then politely said good night and drove home. Honestly, that was all that happened with our first formal date.

Okay, Charlotte and I are adults; both of us had gone through bad divorces at just about the same time. We're adults in this, the second decade of the 21st century ... but for our view of ethics and faith, let's just say that there are some things that are indeed private and I will not write about. If you who are reading this find that disappointing, then I suggest getting some fifty shades of whatever type of book. Granted, that wild intoxicating chemistry and desire are part of what we all are, but if you are looking to read about it here you've got the wrong book.

Two days later, we had a Friday night date which I define as "Our First Elegant Date."

At six foot four in height, I had a wonderful advantage. The small window in the door where Charlotte was living at the time started at just about six feet high. So just standing on my toes on her porch, I looked in and smiled, and the sight of her approaching was stunning; she was in a lovely dress. The door opened, then a moment of just both of us staring at each other, unable to speak.

Dinner was at the Grove Park which is *the* elegant place for a Friday night in Asheville, North Carolina. There is something about elegant surroundings, a magnificent view of our mountains, and most of the patrons dressed well and behaving politely that just fit perfectly.

I should add that we are most definitely not the country club types. I grew up working class; my neighborhood was mostly immigrants from post World War Europe and first generation Americans, hard working and proud. Unfortunately, that enclave was surrounded by one of the wealthiest suburbs of New York City and the silver-spoon brats from that end of town gave me a lifelong disdain for the spoiled nouveau-riche. Besides, I can't stand the game of golf even though I sweated for four years working as an assistant greenskeeper. My definition of a country club? A grass strip airport smelling of aviation gas, oil, old planes, and salt-of-the-earth pilots who are in love with the dream of flying. But once in awhile, I do enjoy a touch of class ... a chance for both of us to dress up and go out on the town.

As the maître d' led us to our table, I, of course, held Charlotte's chair to help her sit and the look she gave me was that look that, even as I write this, still sends shivers down my spine. I sat down across from her and ordered two glasses of champagne. She looked at me a bit wide-eyed and said, "You are the first man who has ever helped me with my chair."

Was I really that "Old School?" I wondered. It was something my father had taught me to do for my mother; it was just part of how a man treated any lady. Feminism be damned!

We have today a couple of generations of men who are terrified to open a door and step aside for a woman, afraid to address someone as "ma'am," or to offer a hundred other gestures of deference, out of fear of being harassed, publicly denounced and perhaps, behind the scenes, suffer anonymous professional attacks. I dated (briefly, very briefly) one extremist who blew a gasket because, when out with her and her spoiled daughter, I insisted upon paying for some candy and opening doors for them. Frankly, I love such traditions which make a twin flame relationship stronger and more respectful. So tell me, what is wrong with a man being deferential and respectful?

With that said, back to the events of that mystical

night.

After a wonderful dinner, the conversation glowing bright, we left the restaurant and went for a stroll around the ground floor of that magnificent old hotel. Charlotte excused herself to go to the rest room and I just stood out in the hallway, looking out at the city of Asheville, all lit up on a sparkly early winter night. And then it really happened, the getting hit-by-a-Mack truck kind of moment.

My back was turned to the corridor and to her as she left the rest room and started to walk towards me but her image was reflected in the window.

Time distorted out, everything passing in slow motion. She was walking towards me, not able to see that I was watching her reflection in the window. She was absolutely radiant, and the way she was looking at me ... not knowing that I was watching her every move, the way she walked, the feminine sway of her body, the intoxicating smile ... a David Lean romantic movie from the 1960s couldn't begin to rival that moment. It was the moment I knew this truly was my twin flame, that she was falling in love with me as I had fallen in love with her.

TWIN FLAME

Chapter Three Narration:
Synchronicity

It was a level of synchronicity when Grant put his hand up to Charlotte's in the vulcan mating ritual. As their fingers touched in a geometric complement, so did their souls. The Trekkie Vulcans control their emotionalism with logic which is well known. In the Star Trek series we learn that the Vulcans have the urge to court every seven years or perish. It is more of a symbolic end of existence that might occur for Grant and Charlotte but the positive thoughts of this narrator see a metaphor of similarity between the mating rituals of both the twin flames and the Vulcans. Pon farr comes complete with many of the emotional swings experienced by twin flame phases. Watching the Bounty episode confirms that for Vulcans biology overcomes rational control in a vast hormonal surge, the feverish compulsion to court, right along side of the irritability and irrational emotions of anger at the loved one. The twin flame dance in fact only differs in one respect, which is the length of the courtship far exceeding the seven days, to the enlightenment and ultimate joy of the relationship.

"Synchronicity" is a captivating word but defined differently by people. It's not all that complicated to define a concept like synchronicity but far superior is the use of example. An example that depicts no obvious causal relationship between events or series of messages that are leading the individual, but unknown to the individual at the same time. It can be very confusing until seen in retrospect. Carl Jung, the world famous psychiatrist, coined the use of the word synchronicity as a concept during the early 1900s.

A young child requests piano lessons at age twelve.

She promises to study hard and convinces the parents she will never need to be told to practice her lessons. Something about her intensity motivates her father to pay the local music teacher to provide instruction. The child's musical passion is combined with talent, but lessons are expensive so they are put on hold. The wonderful woman who is her first teacher provides one final free lesson and teaches her prodigy to play Vivaldi's Four Seasons Le Quattro Stagioni as if she were a world class musician. They play Winter for Four Hands, Quattro. It is exhilarating and our young pianist memorizes the sheet music for a duet that will be a major part of her life. As the youngster exits the music studio after that last lesson she is met with a soft rain and can't for the moment decide if it is a tear running down her face at the disappointment of no future lessons, but the sun shines brightly and a small but magnificent rainbow appears.

The mother of our young musician in the making suggests she study the flute in the sixth grade where the lessons are free and the instrument can be rented. The point is made that learning to read music is the goal at this point anyway. The end result is a smashing blow to a young pianist-to-be but she complies and learns the basics of what we suspect will be a career in the world of music.

Fast forward to high school and the young teen who loved the piano has taught herself to read music, write lyrics and has, before age fifteen, written several original pieces. Her passionate flame for the piano now includes a part time job enabling her to pay for her own private lessons. Unfortunately life and finances get in the way at about this point and divert all of her energy to the field hockey team that her dad assures her will result in a full athletic scholarship and free ride to college.

And so it was that on that one night the future half of a

twin flame is sitting in her dorm with nothing but a dumb reality show to watch or accept the invitation of a sorority sister and attend a free concert. She opts for the concert, expecting the usual ear drum shattering music of a hard rock band with the only relief from the high decibels coming when the musicians proselytize their pet political rhetoric of the month. Much of that dribble being in opposition to her work ethic and family values.

The walk to the concert will take about fifteen minutes and there is a slight misty rain falling. She opts to walk quickly, allowing the rain to coat her face which elicits days, long ago, of puddle jumping as a child. The nimbus clouds break and just at that moment before cumulous puffs float in, there is a rainbow. She smiles as we all do at the sight of a magnificent rainbow and, thinking nothing more than how blessed her life was at that moment, she heads into the concert building.

The amphitheater is silent and only half full. The student feels the hair on the back of her neck stand at attention as the pianist takes his seat. It is a wonderful turn of events and she is thrilled that she attended. The young musician is totally in awe and she is breathless at the sight of both the musician and the man. He seems familiar, perhaps one of the guys who pops up in her many dreams. This man is muscular, blond, blue-eyed and brilliant as he plays his first piece. It is one she has played many times but as she listens she falls in love, with him, his musical expertise, his look. He is older and has a mature presence. She is lost in the chords and melody of her pianist, loving every moment. As he returns for one more piece she tenses, sitting at the edge of her seat as she hears and remembers the first time she also played Winter for Four Hands, Quattro.

In what seems like minutes the evening concert ends

and, standing on her chair, she shouts, "Bravo!" along with many others in attendance. The pianist exits the stage and she feels a sense of remorse that she will never meet him or be able to express her appreciation for his gift.

The young woman and the pianist of this meaningful event will in fact meet again in several years and enter the next phase of a lifelong twin flame relationship complete with children, grand children, jobs at a prestigious school of music and all the joys and sorrows of the classic twin flame relationship. Oh yes ... at their wedding they performed a piano duet of the song Vivaldi Four Seasons, bringing new meaning to the idea of "their song" played at most weddings. Preparing the limo for the honeymoon departure the driver says look at that amazing rainbow...

"A soul-mate is an ongoing connection with another individual that the soul picks up again in various times and places over lifetimes. We are attracted to another person at a soul level not because that person is our unique complement, but because by being with that individual, we are somehow provided with an impetus to become whole ourselves."
- Edgar Cayce

Chapter Four

Some Back Story

Perhaps it is time for a little back story. I won't start the way Dickens did with *David Copperfield*, "I was born..." Let's just fast forward twenty years from the first day of my life.

As mentioned earlier I grew up in a working class neighborhood just outside of Newark, New Jersey. Hard working folks were my neighbors and role models. In more than a few neighborhoods, Italian was the language of parents and grandparents. But the kids, they were going to be Americans, get an education, work hard, and be proud of where they came from and who their parents and grandparents dreamed they would become.

My grandfather, whom I absolutely adored, had come over from Germany in 1909 and had worked his entire life in a gas plant. My father would have gone the same route, laboring in a gas plant that cooked coal to turn into gas, except for the war. After that he got a chance at a college education with the GI bill, and eventually got a degree in chemistry to work ... where else, a gas plant! Mom was a traditional stay-at-home mother raising three kids.

I was, and will always be, a nerd. When I was six or seven the school gave me an I.Q. test. I still recall a short time later my sitting in a room with my mother and I guess it was a couple of psychologists doing the, "Make up a story about this picture," "Let's see you put the blocks in the various holes," type of things. Long afterwards I would find out that they were testing me to go to a special school for the gifted at Columbia University. There was even an article about that school in Life Magazine from that time. I found that article just a few years ago, looked at the kids who are my age now and wondered how they turned out. Were they professors at M.I.T., holders of Noble Prizes or instead whacked out? (You look at the odds in our society that are stacked against gifted kids and it is disturbing, a very high percentage wind up as dropouts and trapped in lives of quiet desperation.)

My parents disagreed with the "experts," wanting me to have a normal childhood rather than be in some lab school. How different my path would have been, for better or worse?

Those first tests would haunt me for decades, because by the time I was in eighth grade that same school district was telling my parents that I had a mental disability, that I should be put in a different kind of special class and even held back a year. It wouldn't be until my late twenties, as I mentioned earlier, that I would be diagnosed with severe dyslexia. The dyslexia balanced the I.Q., resulting in a performance that was, at least in the classroom, abysmal. I was a weird kid with problems! But beyond the frustrations, and there were plenty of them for my parents, both knew there was some sort of path I was supposed to take … if they didn't drown me first. (Years later, several days after I called to tell them I had sold my first novel in spite of all the odds stacked against me, my mother sent me a post card and had written on the back, "I am so proud of you." On the front of that card was a quote from Thoreau about marching to the beat of a different drummer. My parents at last understood why.)

So I was a weird kid. Stumbling through school, I had difficulty relating to nearly everyone except one or two close friends. I was a tall, 150-pound, gangly and uncoordinated teenage nerd who was the target of a lot of bullying. Certainly not the formula for a guy to be self-assured when it came to meeting girls. My parents wound up sending me to an all-male Catholic high school in Newark where I spent three miserable years. The happiest day of my life, up to that point, was when I was expelled for academic failure and for making a rude gesture on the last day of my junior year to "Fat Larry" the abbot.

Fortunately a bit of a turnaround occurred the following year. My father had gotten a promotion and we had moved out to the suburbs, to one of those Levittown-type developments sprouting up all over Jersey corn fields in the 1950s and 60s. I wound up in a good school with a couple of incredible teachers who turned my life around, pointing me in the direction of being a history teacher. I even asked a girl to the senior prom, kissed her once (my first kiss) and then suffered the breakup the following day so she could go out with a guy who could imitate "Tiny Tim." If you aren't from the 1960s you don't know who that was, and maybe that's for the best because it was a real ego blow to me.

My point? As Woody Allen would later joke, here I was in the middle of the sexual revolution of the sixties and I was a non-combatant.

Sure, I dated a bit, but it seemed that a lot more of my time was spent reading history, science fiction and, above all else, Heinlein, Bradbury and Tolkien. I lived in that world and played complex board games about Gettysburg and D-Day with fellow nerds.

A girl finally did wander into the scene, "Mary." She was a history education major like me and she was the one who finally hit me with the legendary "Sicilian Lightning Bolt." It was the start of my junior year in college, in a course on Roman history taught by a wonderful favorite professor. I came in a few minutes early, took a seat a few rows back and waited for class to start.

Mary walked in and sat down directly in front of me. And, though a nerd, I was most definitely a healthy straight male! I could not help but notice her and was absolutely stunned when she turned around in her seat in front of me, looked me straight in the eye with her baby blues, and said something about how great the professor was. That was it ... I was smitten.

I think all of us can, or at least should be able to, smile decades later about the wonder, mystery, fear and delight of that first infatuation. We can analyze it long after the pain is over to see all that was wrong and, like that whole Kubler-Ross thing about the stages of grief, you gradually get through the hurt and denial, and then on to acceptance. And finally to a bit of a smile as you think, "Thank God that didn't work out!"

Not to denigrate Mary. Just because one finally realizes, perhaps years later, that your first infatuation is not your twin flame does not mean there is something wrong with the other person. I have come to believe that for everyone there is indeed a twin flame. The problem, of course, is finding him or her I have a deep sense of faith but I did wish at times that God had made the journey easier.

I was awed by Mary in the way a nerdy and lonely twenty-year-old can be awed. She was considered to be one of the most stunningly attractive girls on my campus. Wherever she went, nearly every guy would sprain his neck turning to look at her. She had something of an innocent demeanor, of just walking on, not aware, at least consciously, of the sprained necks, auto wrecks, and plane crashes left in her wake.

Her? Interested in me, the campus nerd? Nah, never a chance, but I did worship her from afar and given that we had the same major, we were sharing several classes that semester, so our paths crossed daily. Towards the end of the semester I was up late in the library, working on a paper for Roman history. It was actually one of my first serious attempts at creative writing. The wonderful professor in that class, understanding that I had some sort of learning disability but had a serious knowledge of the subject anyway, gave me a lot of latitude. He approved my writing a fictional story, but based on fact: the life story of a Roman soldier, from recruitment out of the slums of Rome, to retirement after thirty years' service in the Civil Wars and garrisoning the frontier with Germania.

Mary walked by, of course I sprained my neck, my heart racing as she stopped, smiled, and asked me what I was working on. I was stunned when she then asked if she could read it. I guess it was one of my very first critical reviews outside of so many teachers who had scrawled red marks all over the pages (I flunked college English twice … remember, dyslexia)!

I was expecting just a polite "that's nice" response. Mary was the type of girl who was always polite to the swarm of guys who were hovering about and then would move on. But instead she was praising my imagination. It turned into an hour or so, even walking to the student union for coffee, talking about history.

So thus it started, our talking after class. I even walked her to her dorm a few times, but never made a move. I mean, who was I? A nerd and she was very much something of the queen of the campus. But unlike so many campus queens, she did not belong to a sorority. She was intelligent, a gentle soul, and extremely attractive.

The semester ended, and I spent Christmas at home kicking myself that I had not worked up the nerve to at least get her address and phone number.

There was only one campus activity that I was darn

good at: chess. I was a fanatical and highly aggressive player. The chess club on campus was informal. What guy in his right mind wanted to be openly associated with a chess club? So we nerds would meet in a corner of the library several times a week for some games which I almost always won. One day at the start of the Spring semester I was talking with Mary about the game and she finally broke the ice.

"Would you teach me to play?" she asked, again hitting me with those baby blue eyes and innocent gaze, and a minute later she suggested tea and chess for that Friday night in her dorm room.

Talk about staggered! Was this a date? Or was it a "just be friends" type of thing?

It was Friday night and I showered twice, shaved to the point of more than a few nicks, put on too much deodorant, and took care of those dang zits that had to pop up that morning. I was soon after at the front desk of her dorm.

How life in college was changing during those four years! That would be the last year that a gentleman caller, or some heavy-handed frat boy still had to sign in at the front desk. The girl would be paged, and she would come down to meet you. Rules had changed enough that a guy could go up to her room but still, at midnight he was to be out the door.

Of course being paged like that, and heading up several floors, every girl there was checking out who Mary was "taking upstairs." It was the first time I had ever actually been in a girl's dorm.

She already had the chess board out, tea brewing, I sat down nervously on the bed, set up the pieces and I guess it was an hour or two of explaining the game and sipping tea. I was nervous as all hell. This had to be a, "Let's be friends" type of thing. Me, the nerd?

And then it hit. I had just explained some sort of move, the Sicilian Gambit, the Mafia Left Hook, I don't know. She looked straight at me, smiled, and said, "Grant, how come you've never tried to kiss me?"

Duh, gee, gosh ... I couldn't say a word.

She pushed the chess board aside, leaned over and kissed me like I had never been kissed before.

Okay, enough with that, time to shift the scene.

It was a mad infatuation that lasted for a year and a half and would haunt me for forty years afterwards. I thought I had found my soul mate (I had no idea yet or for a long time to come about the far deeper meanings of twin flames). Of course it didn't work out. I wasn't her soul mate nor she mine.

The breakup came after we graduated from college. I had refused to accept that for her it had lasted the several months of that Spring semester. After a summer apart, her working at a camp in upstate New York, my cutting greens on a golf course and getting up at three in the morning to run the irrigation system, we were already drifting apart.

This was the world before the Internet, texting and tweeting. It was still written letters and long distance phone calls, with her feeding quarters into the one phone at the camp that was available to the staff. Returning to college that fall I thought it would all be the same but already it was not. When you are twenty sometimes reality has to punch you square between the eyes before you finally see it.

We were supposedly still a couple for that senior year, at least I thought we were. It would come out that she did not. Graduation came and went, me back at the golf course, desperately searching for a teaching job which would not finally surface until six years later, her at the summer camp again and then off to graduate school in the fall. She came back from camp and finally let the bomb drop ... it was over and she was going with someone else.

That summer and autumn right out of college was a rotten time all around. The market for teaching jobs had completely collapsed in 1972 as the peak wave of the baby boom generation had grown up. Strange to see now that my entire world up to that moment had been living in New Jersey, the furthest I had even traveled up to that time was a trip to Civil War battlefields in Virginia that my parents took me on when I was fourteen. In order to pay for that trip my mom had worked, babysitting and cleaning houses, and my dad had sacrificed most of his two-week vacation. It was the trip that had cemented my lifelong interest in military history and the Civil War. How profound such things are, when done by loving parents, that set the trajectory of one's life.

I had lived with the fantasy that I would graduate college, find a teaching job in Jersey, and marry Mary. The thought of it now, over forty years later ... my guardian angels knew it would have to be different even when I could not see it.

The path to your twin flame is strewn with pain. It is part of what makes your twin flame even more precious when at last found.

So it was goodbye to Mary, with a lot of tears and a lot of sleepless nights. It took two years for the pain to subside.

I mentioned that she haunted me, and she did. You move on with your life, and, after the pain burns itself out, you feel that what is left within is an empty dark void that can never be filled again. You look back. You replay all of the "should haves" and you wonder, "Why?"

If you, reading this now, are at that moment of pain

and asking God, "Why?" perhaps it is to learn just how precious life truly is, to live each moment fully, but also to learn that in that burning away of the past it is perhaps God's way of preparing you for what shall come.

I am a historian, my business is the past. It is so easy to romanticize it. But to try to actually live it again, or imagine what it really was like? PBS had a series some years back of taking a family for a few months, and, except for emergency backup, they lived the past as it was: a nice house in Victorian 1890. After four weeks all of the participants were ready to kill for real soap, flushing toilets, central heating and air conditioning, and a Big Mac sandwich with fries and a soda.

Isn't the same true of memories in our own lives where we wash away the hurt until at times there is just a soft glow of lost days? So yes, she did trouble my memories, and, truthfully, did so until a day in November of 2013.

That fact that all wistful memory of Mary disappeared on that November day was one of the big giveaways that I had met my twin flame at last. The memory of what I had come to believe was the one brief moment of absolute true happiness faded away, and slipped out of my heart forever.

So in closing on this part of the story, thank you, Mary, and I wish you well with sincere hope that you did at last find your twin flame, for it was definitely not to be us.

With that now written down, how to cover the rest of this back story for I certainly did not live alone, in solitude like someone from a Gordon Lightfoot song who believes he will never have "that feeling" ever again?

I did marry. Actually twice, each marriage lasting a dozen years. For Charlotte there would be one broken marriage before we met.

What to put into writing and what to leave behind?

Surely if we married so many years ago it was with the belief that it would be for a lifetime. Did we not feel confident that this was the love of our life? Well ... yes and no.

Did it seem like the right thing to do at the time? Of course, for if not it was morally wrong, especially in relationship to the one you are marrying. But was there wondering later? Most certainly yes.

I'll not write or speak negatively of either of the women I married before meeting Charlotte, nor analyze what was right and what was definitely wrong. Yes there was the "impulse of delight" that led to marriage, even a belief that it would be a good life to share together.

But then again, and this might be painful for some who read this ... was there not a wondering at times?

Have you ever had a moment of stark realization? You wake up at three in the morning from a dream you can't quite remember. You can only recollect that it was deeply troubling. You look over at the person asleep beside you. Of course there is a warmth, a love, for after all, you are married. But then again there is something that just doesn't quite seem to fit together. There is no thought of just shrugging off whatever the dream was and snuggling closer beside that person, returning to peaceful sleep.

No, instead you lie there awake ... troubled, even confused, and at times frightened ... is this really my life?

A comparison to at least one dream that happened to me. I was lying in a field at night looking up at the stars and the thinking kicked in. Just how vast the universe is. If a nerd, you might even know that the light from a particular pinpoint sparkling above took a hundred years to reach your eyes and register. That is longer than you've been alive! Then that one over there, just below Orion's Belt, that is a hundred thousand or more light years away, a cluster of tens of thousands of stars. You start thinking about it all: the time, the distance, the vastness and then ... oh my gosh, stop!

If you keep it up much longer you're going to slip back into some idiotic philosophy class discussion of what is reality and it is all too vast. It gets too deep and best to just leave it to God. To continue to pursue the thoughts racing through your mind actually become overwhelming and frightening ... so you bury them back deep into your subconscious.

Maybe that little segway might explain those three-in-the–morning, wide awake thoughts, "Is this really my life? And am I really happy with the person I am with?" Those type of moments have you backing away from allowing the thoughts to continue and overwhelm you.

You finally fall back asleep, awaken in the morning, and push the thoughts aside. You ask your spouse, how did she sleep? You gulp down a cup of coffee and then fall back into work and the routines of life. You try not to think about how vast the universe is in comparison to you, about your momentary existence here, or is that person sitting across from you really truly your twin Flame with a love that transcends all the questions about our brief moment of life and the eternity before and the eternity afterwards?

Both marriages would fail, and no comment here as to the hows, the whys, the whos are to blame and, during those darkest moments, the anger that burns away all memory of what first brought you together.

The one blessing from the second marriage was a remarkable daughter whom I would go on to raise on my own from the time she was thirteen ... perhaps another book someday about the eternal relationship between parent and child.

As to the haunting by Mary? Yes, it was there. It would disappear for a time, even years, but then as the cracks in the facade of a marriage grew wider, there would be a wondering ... was that moment of happiness known as an idealistic twenty-year-old really all that would ever be?

A very depressing thought, that one. To think that your fate might very well be to never truly find that lifelong joy. There was guilt as well for, after all, was I not married to someone else, so why the troubling memories of someone else? Or was it a deeper realization that no one wants to have surface: that something is missing and it will never be completely whole?

I can recall one such moment so clearly years after Mary had stepped out of my life. I was walking through snow covered woods after a blizzard and was hit with the memory of having done the same with Mary. I sat down alone in the frozen silent woods, recalling a hike with Mary to a frozen waterfalls on a similar day when the snow blanketed the ground, flurries still drifting down, the rest of the world disappearing except for the two of us. There was a visceral recollection of that moment when I had felt so intensely alive and happy beyond anything I had ever felt before.

Recalling it, I sat in the woods and cried.

But then? A walk back home where someone else was now the partner in my life, someone I deeply cared for, but for whom that type of magical intensity simply was not there. Talk about a flood of guilt as I trudged back home, snow drifting down like a curtain to seal off the tears I had just shed. I was telling myself over and over, "I'm married to someone else, live life as it is and accept what is."

If you want to know a certain clear giveaway that you have found your twin flame, walk with her on a snowy day, or in a driving rain, sit by her side in front of a fire on a foggy November morning and as you do so, know with absolute certainty that there is no one else in the world, past, present or future, with whom you would rather share that moment. You have that … you have your twin flame.

A confession … I'm a sucker for several romantic movies. I think most guys are, as long as it is not something by Nicolas Sparks. For me it was *Portrait of Jennie*, made in 1948 with Jennifer Jones and Joseph Cotton. I remember seeing it for the first time when I was seventeen or so, and it blew me away. The plot: a lonely artist walking through Central Park meets a very young Jennifer Jones, her winter clothing dated from thirty years earlier and not of the time that the artist was living in.

It finally is revealed that she is a ghost, born out of the sequence of time from the artist. In the months that follow she haunts his every waking moment. They meet several more times, and each time she is older, and each time she tells him that she is growing up so that they can then be together forever. Each time she looks at him with her soulful gaze telling him that she is waiting for him. Mystery and fascination give way to a deep, all-consuming love that inspires the artist to transcend all of his previous work as he paints her portrait: thus, the title of the movie. But remember, she is a ghost, the artist finally learns that this mysterious young woman had died years ago. No spoiler here … buy a copy, watch it, and you'll understand why it has stayed with me. For I wondered so many hundreds of times, "Is that my story? But for me I will not even, at least in this lifetime, meet the ghost of the one who really is my twin flame.

But I finally did.

That is why I wrote this chapter, to put the past perspective on why I so joyfully and fully embraced that which was to come: the good times, and yes, there will be some tough times as well, for that is what life is.

Chapter Four Narration:
Escaping the Early Relationships as a Learning Process

Virtually all soul mates have experienced a point in the vagaries of the relationship where some disagreement or disappointment results in one of the partners threatening or abandoning the other partner. Disagreements escalate to fighting and feelings of despair creep in that the partner will not to listen to requests for compromise. It is the moment of choice where the one most unhappy with what seems like endless fighting will always continue and for the most part experience repetition of prior failure to communicate, decides to exit. It is the great escape, and in the mind of one partner the only way to survive the pain of being in the relationship. The escape is complete with a fight to end all fights when bridges are burned and things are said in an attempt to feel justified in what is about to happen. The end is near or so the twin flame thinks and the scorched earth policy is the battle plan.

It might start like any night, he barbecues and she washes the dishes. She decides to do some knitting while he watches the game. In between the popcorn and milkshakes one of them has a burning desire to make a point. Those three simple words will alter the course of the relationship forever. The man is mesmerized by the athletic event, but the woman wants to talk. The moment is met with a suggestion to wait until halftime.

By the time half time comes around the tension in the room is palpable. She needs to make a point about the way he drives her car without ever refilling the gas tank. He finds the point being made another dissatisfaction in a long line of complaints, attacking his style and method of operation. She escalates and pushes harder on her point to her painful areas of her ex controlling her credit cards and in the process preventing her from even using the car. He shouts back that he is not her ex. Cut to hours of shouting about everything from dropping dirty clothes in the middle of the floor to failure to clean up a cluttered kitchen.

The surprise in the escape is not the woman walking out in a final this is really the end moment but rather the man. The woman wanted to make a point, the man listened and let it play out and then he left. He left with such finality that she was sure she would never see him again. In silence he packs his car leaving some things of little significance and believing there is no way resolve the issues. She is certain it is a stunt and probably waits up all night expecting a reconciliation. It doesn't work that way. He is gone and she sits alone in their home unable to communicate in any way. He has blocked all forms of communication and makes it clear over the next few days it is over. She gets angry and triangulates though a third party who will reach him with her concept of the break up.

What is really happening here is the escape by a runner which comes when he doesn't feel heard. It can be a man or a woman who runs and within a certain amount of time, the other will make tireless attempts to find him and request or even beg for one more chance. It doesn't happen that easily and months go by with both in agony because both remember they are twin flames trying to find their way back to each other. He is miserable without her so he drinks more than normal and neglects his job. She searches the Internet for an intellectual basis for his behavior and tries to analyze why this happened. They both blame other people, other friends, family, medications, alcohol and their parents for their child rearing. They wait and hope and finally as the awakening occurs begin to remember whom they love.

"The ultimate lesson all of us have to learn is unconditional love, which includes not only others but ourselves as well."
- Elizabeth Kubler-Ross

Dr. Elizabeth Kubler-Ros was heavily influenced by the relief work she did after WWII at a former Nazi death camp in Poland known as Maidanek. It is suggested that her theories on the stages of grief were formulated in her early years after graduating from medical school. She married and divorced after two decades. He remarried, she did not. When asked directly how the stages of grief applied to her break up and divorce, the honesty of her answer shocked the world. She said, "I am in the angry phase ... I'm pissed!"

TWIN FLAME

Chapter Five

~

Memories of Dating Past

I think it is time for something a little less heavy. Such a great 1960s and 70s term, that phrase, "Wow man, that's heavy!" Marty McFly uses it a lot in *Back to the Future*, much to the confusion of those whom he meets in the past. When I recall the path to my twin flame that phrase comes to mind as the best way to describe it all: wow, that was heavy.

These are a few tales of the "between the marriages" dating world. For those of you who have been through the turmoil of divorce I suspect it will bring a smile or a shaking of your head with your muttering, "Yeah that was heavy, or freaky, or what a bummer..." I have learned, though, that all of it is part and parcel of that quest for the twin flame.

Most of this will be about the bizarre dating world created by the Internet, but a few tales before that time are in order.

I believe that the pattern of behavior after a divorce falls into a few distinct categories. The first one: running amok. You are out the far side of a divorce and what are friends urging you to do? Run amok. "Hey, you're free, buddy, and I know this girl who..." Fill in the blanks for the rest of that sentence, be you male or female, which a sure path to shallowness and lifelong regrets.

Whatever the motivation for that first date, one finally comes your way: The First Date after a divorce. You go out, you think you feel free, at least for a moment, from the past. But the divorce lingers, either with tears or anger. Memory of that other person is sitting right there with you.

The result is usually a disastrous evening, especially if the other person is in the same life boat of recovery.

Perhaps then you withdraw, you spend a lot of nights of staring at the ceiling and, I'll confess, more than a few nights watching some television program and talking with a bottle of scotch. For me, there was, as well, solace to be found in turning out a few more books. When into The Zone of writing, at least everything else, especially the loneliness, disappears for awhile. And then you finally try again.

A couple of memories of the "get back out there and try again" phase of life. A big factor for most of us, your ever-present, helpful friends… "I know the perfect girl for you, she works in my office, I told her all about you, she is way hot…"

So you agree to meet.

Memory of two such dates stand out sharply, even now. The first one, I was in grad school and newly divorced. A friend said she knew the perfect girl. I agreed to try the waters of the infamous "blind date set up by matchmaking friends."

My friend gave me "Alice's" phone number. I called, we chatted a bit, it seemed okay, and we agreed to meet at a local Chinese restaurant, her in a red dress and driving a white car.

I draw the analogy that such things are like a combat marine going into yet another hostile beach. High command is telling you that this will be a cakewalk. Just get out of the landing craft and walk ashore, to be greeted by joyful natives. But prior experience? The landing craft blows up and sinks, the natives are not just unfriendly, they are actually somewhat crazy. Or is it you who is crazy after all?

I got to the parking lot outside the restaurant a few

minutes early and, sure enough, a white car pulls up. Out steps a woman wearing a red dress and, oh my gosh, my friend was right! This is one darn attractive woman. Hey maybe this time something will work! (Of course, I was a typical male, too often judging by looks even before she opened her mouth to speak.)

I got out of the car, put on my best, Hi, I'm-glad–to-meet-you smile, and walk up to her. She turns and smiles a bit nervously.

"Hi, I'm Grant, are you Alice?"

And with that, the smile broadened, a bit of a laugh, and then, "No, my name is Rachel." A pause followed. "I bet you are here on a blind date."

Oh. My. Gosh. Talk about humiliation. No one wants to admit he is so desperate that he would actually sink to a blind date!

Rapid apologies were fired off, followed by retreat as that wonderfully attractive woman walked off. Then another white car pulled up, out stepped the real Alice and, sigh, you know what I mean. There is either chemistry or there isn't and, even before she opened her mouth, I knew this was going to be one bummer of a date. The dinner was polite but wooden, a stumbling about that even talking about the weather was a stretch followed by long silences.

This is the sad part of the entire dating experience. You do meet a lot of nice people, but there are more than a few nut jobs, and a few who set off alarms to end the date as swiftly as possible, go back to the television and the bottle of scotch. And as I write this I wonder now about the memories of those I met … am I remembered now as the "nice guy who got away?" or perhaps for some I was "a real nut job!"

A lasting memory of that first blind date. The first woman I had met was sitting across the restaurant and facing my direction. The guy she was with was a rather loud-mouthed jerk. There were more than a few eye contacts between that other woman and me. Alice and I got up to leave and as I walked past girl number one, I had a momentary temptation. Should I pull out a card, hand it to her and walk on? I didn't, but I actually did wonder later about that path not taken. As for Alice, a nice girl, and yeah, that uncomfortable phone call a day later, the, "I'll call you tomorrow," thing. How I hate that. Alice was a nice person, but definitely a no-starter.

Case study two of "friends who just want to help."

I got a phone call from a friend and his wife. They were very excited, on their way back from a trip to Atlanta, and proudly announced that, "We've found you something incredible, meet us for dinner in an hour!"

Something incredible from Atlanta? Remember I'm a Civil War historian and I collect artifacts. Wow! Friends are picking up Civil War related stuff for me all the time, usually a book or one of those fake newspapers about Gettysburg. But this couple know that I was a serious collector. Gosh, maybe they were coming back with something like an artillery shell!

I actually raced to where they said we should meet. They were there ahead of me. I walked in and ... it sure wasn't an artillery shell ... it was a bomb. Not a bombshell, just a bomb, the type that is ticking and you darn well better run!

My friends had carted a woman all the way up from Atlanta to meet me. Less than a minute later I was contemplating murder. This was not mixing gunpowder with a match for a neat explosion. I could come up with a lot of other analogies beyond impolite.

When I met Charlotte, that first touch, just brushing against each other, was a delightful electric shock, but this? I assume a lot of you have had such a moment where the other person has her hand on your forearm within seconds after meeting and you want to recoil. I had to sit next to this person for a half hour who was instantly all over me. I've talked with many a woman who can describe with a facial wrinkle of disdain how they met a guy who, within minutes, was leering at her, trying to paw at her and attempting to run a hand up her thigh. Well it can happen to a guy too, and that was such a moment. She claimed to be a fan of my books, freaked out when my friends mentioned knowing me and insisted that they bring her back to meet me, and they gladly complied. The subtext was clear within minutes … some late night entertainment was to follow.

It was one of those moments where my tendency to be polite just snapped. A hand brushing up over my knee had me suddenly standing up, dropping a twenty dollar bill on the table to pay for a dinner that had yet to arrive and, without excuse, announcing that I was out of there.

My friends actually had the nerve to call me back an hour later with news that my "artillery shell" was staying the night with them and why don't I come over for a drink … wink, wink, nudge, nudge? I'll refrain from writing down my reply before I hung up five seconds later.

Some people, especially women I know, describe the dating scene as feeling like you are in a meat market. That experience taught me about their side of the "wonderful world of dating, thanks to friends."

How about the "random encounter that seems ordained by fate, but quickly turns to hell?"

It was a summer, twenty-five years ago, having just finished up an intense two years for my master's degree and that fall I headed straight into a Ph.D. program. Along with other interests of my life, I am a fanatical eclipse chaser. That summer an eclipse was destined to cross central Mexico, including Tenochtilan, what had once been the capital of the Aztecs: the same guys who regularly tore out human hearts as sacrifices to their gods (maybe a bit of a metaphor there for my life at that time).

Amtrak was running a $150 special pass for students: travel anywhere for three weeks. I did a bit of checking and found out that I could travel down to Mexico for only a hundred dollars more, first class no less rather than coach, aboard a Mexican train.

So off I went on a three-week adventure to chase an eclipse and maybe I might even meet *her*.

The professional advice on seeing the eclipse was to head down to the west coast of Mexico to Mazatlan, where there was a 90% chance of good weather, instead of climbing up the pyramid in Tenochtilan where there was a 90% chance of clouds (and also a 10% chance that someone might rip your heart out when the eclipse went total).

So there I was, two weeks later, staring up at a cloud obscuring the sun as the eclipse went total, but the show was surreal nevertheless as I watched the shadow wall racing in from the Pacific. The cold wind swept in from the sea as the world went dark, eliciting a chilled fear. It really triggered a sense of primordial dread no matter how well versed you are in modern astronomy. Then, later that day I headed down to the train station for the two-day ride back to the States.

I was traveling lightly with the usual student backpack and walked into the sweltering hot, fly-splattered station and, right there, it happened. It was just like the opening scene in the movie, *Leave Her to Heaven*, which starts with a beautiful woman played by Gene Turney reading a novel by, who else, the main character. (Spoiler alert: she later murders his brother, commits suicide, and frames him to make it look like he killed her!)

So here was this stunningly beautiful woman, mid to late twenties, curled up on one of those old-fashioned railroad station benches, absolutely absorbed in, you got it: one of my novels!

At this stage in my career I was just beginning to crawl out of the sci-fi ghetto where I had been consigned by my first editor, who, when he had published my first novel, had put me at the bottom of his list where I would languish for years, typecast as a sci-fi paperback writer. For seven years he had kept promising, "Next book you're going to get the big push," and it had taken nearly two decades to escape from that ditch. Maybe someday a book about the politics of the publishing industry is in order: who gets that "push," whether the book deserves it or not, and who gets the boot to the bottom.

A few years prior to this meeting in the railroad station, a good friend, a fellow author who at that time was flourishing, had given me straight advice. He had introduced me to the agent with whom I have been now for over twenty-five years. She had begun to guide me out of the "ghetto" and, at that moment, I was in middle ground. I had launched a new series with a new publisher, a really great guy, and was actually seeing my sci-fi stories about a Civil War regiment on another world begin to get some kind of readership.

When the publisher's art department designed the covers for the series, they actually recruited me for a bit of an inside joke. I posed for the artist as the Union soldier who would be plastered across the front cover, flanked on the other side by one of the aliens whom I would claim was my cousin Luigi from Jersey City and not to be crossed.

So there was the second book in that series in a beautiful woman's hands, in a godforsaken, out-of-the-way train station in Mexico, with a picture of me on the cover. We were the only two people in that cavernous, sweltering room. Was this God setting me up at last?

Make your move casual, don't frighten her, I thought. (My guardian angels at this moment? Chuckling to themselves as they looked down at the impending tragedy. Their crowning achievement was still twenty-two years away. So for them, this encounter was pure entertainment.) I ambled around the waiting room for a minute or two, sighing, taking off my backpack, wiping my brow in that near hundred degree heat, and looking at the bulletin board as if I could actually read Spanish. Then I finally circled around towards the bench.

I caught a quick glance up from her, a slight nod of, "Yeah, I see you, and no, I'm not interested," then her eyes went back to the book ... to stuff that I had actually written. She, a beautiful woman obviously alone in a foreign train station, undoubtedly had to fend off guys all the time. But this time? Boy was she in for a surprise! It couldn't get any better than this!

I walked past her, feigned a casual glance and then turned as if seeing the cover of the book for the first time.

"Good book?" I asked.

Hmmm, definitely a standard pickup line. The response was expected.

"Yeah, it's good," then her eyes were back to the page as a brush off. (Up over my head my guardian angels were cracking up as they watched the show.)

"Read anything else by that author?"

A bit dangerous, that. She could have said no, or "I lost Stephen King's latest book and found this one in the trash, so I'm killing time with it."

But no!

She looked up at me, another one with those baby blues, and at last a polite smile.

"I've read all his stuff; he's my favorite author."

Oh my gosh! Jackpot! This is it! This is better than the lottery! What a story this will make!

I allowed a polite pause, I didn't move away. A bit of a confused look crossed her face of, "Who is this guy? There's always some strange creep wandering around train stations in Mexico."

I offered a friendly smile and then just two well thought-out words that I conjured up within a second.

"Thank you."

Perplexed, she said nothing, just staring at me.

"I'm the author," I finally continued, with the right savior faire.

Now there was real confusion.

Being all-so–poised, I leaned over the side of the bench, and pointed to my heroic image on the cover. The artist had done a superb job of giving me that hardened hero look, defiantly gazing off to some distant horizon, unafraid of anything that fate might throw at me.

"That's me," and at the same time I pulled out my wallet, opened it and got out my driver's license, the portrait not as heroic but definite proof.

She turned the book, examined the cover, looked up at me as I drew off my thick glasses (when poising as a heroic Civil War soldier one does not wear glasses), then gazed at my driver's license. He eyes went wide and, at last, she spoke.

"Oh my God…!" and she said my name, my full nom de plume author's name.

I just smiled, extended my hand and, in my best Cary Grant style, simply said "My name's Grant and I'm pleased to meet you."

And in those first thirty seconds she went absolutely ecstatic. "I can't believe this ... Oh my God, my favorite author ... what are you doing here ... this is so wild!"

Yup it was wild all right. In movies this kind of stuff happens to authors all the time, usually in the first five minutes of the film. So maybe it was true at last and to heck with the fact that usually the author or someone winds up dead before the movie ends!

"You waiting for the train back to Tijuana?" I finally asked.

"Yes, and you?"

"The same."

Two whole days to get to know this person, who thinks I'm the greatest author alive. Thank you, God!

And then...

She stood up, grinning with delight, actually behaving like a wide-eyed fan.

"Just a minute, don't move, I'll be right back!"

For a second I thought she was so worked up that she had to take a bathroom break. Instead she ran to the exit, opened the door and shouted: "Hey honey get in here now, you're not going to believe who's here!"

What?! No, it can't be! For a split second I harbored a lingering hope ... maybe it's a female friend named Honey or Babette ... or ... or ...

If you have ever been to a sci-fi or Star Trek convention, or even if you haven't, the majority of the stereotypes are true. It is a nerd's paradise and remember, I'm a nerd. But there are nerds and then there are *nerds*. The guy who came bursting through the door at her summons was the archetype of all archetypes of a nerd.

He came waddling through the door, breathing hard, sweat dripping from his face and staining his collar and armpits. She shouted out my name. He slowed for a second, went wide-eyed, and came running up while extending a sweaty paw and with no sense of personal space so I could smell two days' worth of Mexican food on his breath.

And then the torture began.

That torture would last for two whole days, including a long four-hour stretch in 110-degree heat with the asthmatic locomotive breaking down and waiting for a replacement to rescue us while the nerd of nerds rattled on and on: "On page 137 of book one you had a guy get his hand blown off, but on page 93 of book two his hand is back. What happened, did he get a new hand put on like Luke Skywalker in Return of the Jedi? Which is it?"

I'm not making this stuff up; reality really is weirder than fiction.

And yeah, for those two days and long afterwards I wondered, "Is this really the story of my life?" And I also had a profound philosophical pondering. "Does God have a sense of humor?" Some of you might remember Gary Larson of *The Far Side* comic? One of my favorites, which at times I wondered was my story in this game of fate, was "God at His Computer." At the bottom of the cartoon, framed inside a computer screen, is a Larson nerd, oblivious and strolling along. Above him some piano movers are looking on with horror, for the rope hoisting the piano up the side of the building has just snapped, the baby grand falling straight down at the oblivious nerd. In the foreground, there is God, his computer has but one key, and written across it, "*Smite*." God's finger is hovering above the key.

So thus was the one and only time that a beautiful woman was in a train station, or on a plane, or in a taxi, or aboard a ship that has just struck an iceberg, and was observed by me reading one of my books.

Adventures in the Cyber World

Years later, a sad second divorce behind me, technology had taken a huge leap forward for us lonely hearts. In its opening stages, with so many promises that here you will meet your real twin flame, was the realm of Internet dating.

Think of it. You write up your profile, write up your wish list, and select some pictures (and of course you make them current and honest)! You cast your net as wide as you want; you can search your hometown or five hundred miles out. Of course I'm going to give it a try! What a brave new world awaited all of us singles when Match, eHarmony and others came on the scene. Sigh...

And I think every person reading this who has tried Internet dating has his or her favorite story: a funny story, a horror story, an "Oh my gosh!" story, or a "What in heaven's name am I doing here?" story.

I tried it on and off for several years and could darn near write a book about it. But this is about twin flames, the path to finding that one, so just a few anecdotes about true failures to launch.

There was the one who contacted me, a newspaper editor in another state, who almost arranged a date to meet, and then spilled that her ex had just tried to kill her by tying her up, throwing her into the backseat of his SUV, and driving it into a levee (yes a levee, I half assumed it was in a Chevy)! The On-Star alarm had saved her life when it had detected that the car was sinking. Police rescued her but then took her to jail because a significant quantity of hard drugs had been found during the rescue. She was getting that cleared up and in two more months, once the baby was born, she'd love to meet me.

Again, seriously, you can't make this stuff up!

Another was a writer and a poet, no less. At least that was how it was advertised on her web page, though the confession would come out later that the books were all self-published. We saw each other several times and I suggested a date with her daughter and mine to go see a show. Afterwards her kid demands some candy from one of those high-priced specialty stores. A few minutes later the tally is up to twenty dollars and we are at the checkout. I'm a guy of the Old School, so I reach past her with a twenty dollar bill and tell the clerk that I'll take care of it. Then I open the door for them as we leave.

A very icy parting occurred on the sidewalk a minute later and, as we walked away, my daughter had a few very choice words about the lack of manners by the woman and her spoiled kid. I shrugged it off, having already decided that this one was a write off. But whammo! I checked my email later that day. I found a scathing feminist tirade about how I had harassed, demeaned, and humiliated her. That, being taller than she (heck I'm taller than 99.9% of the women out there), my gesture of reaching over her was an act of physical intimidation in front of her daughter. My sin was compounded by the fact that I had just taught her daughter all of the wrong lessons from the feminist bible: *never* let a man pay for anything because of the sociological, psychological and implied sexual lessons. It was like something straight out of the feminist bookstore routines in *Portlandia*. I received feedback from a few mutual acquaintances that there was more than a little pathological lying going on when it came to just how many guys she was actually dating.

A few more dates like that finally taught me to just rewrite my entire profile. We live in such an age of political and social divides that, for me, someone with that attitude is a dead-out-of-the-gate situation. Recall the first date that I wrote about with Charlotte? She had made the polite gesture of offering to pay for her half of the meal. I refused and later she would compliment me, that I was a gentleman who was far different from what she was used to going out with. She was also honest up front about whom, if anyone, she might be dating, another rare positive.

Having just endured the alleged writer/poet and her deceptions and feminist tirades, I seriously began to wonder, what the heck is really out there?!?

So I rewrote my profile and made it clear: I'm old school, I'm politically conservative, and I believe in traditional roles. Yes, I am pro-feminist but I see feminism as women being treated equally in careers and before the law. But, and this is a big but, I will open the door for you, help you with your chair, take my hat off, call you ma'am or miss if I do not know you (or cannot remember your name), and bring flowers to you on a regular basis. If you disagree, don't complain when you find yourself out with creeps who think that sex is a score card as payment for a date after they've dodged the dinner bill.

My rewritten profile got me quite a reaction. A flight attendant, who, just before I drove one hundred miles to meet her, accidentally spilled that she was once featured in the infamous "Fly Me" ads of more than forty years ago. I started to count backwards how many years ago that ad ran and, oh my gosh, it had run when I was in high school! And, at the time, definitely made me want to try out "fly me!" (Remember, I was sixteen back then!) I took a closer look at one of the photos she had posted as current and … is that a 707 parked in the background with a Gremlin car in the foreground? A woman who had appeared in a "Fly-Me" ad? It might have been titillating for a sixteen-year-old. But now? I was on a quest, not out for a one night's stand.

But, I had to honor the commitment for a date which I had made for the following night. Frankly, it was heartbreakingly sad. The poor woman was tragically desperate for someone, anyone, to be in her life. I drove her back to her apartment after dinner and politely begged off from the, "Why don't we have a drink?" offer. I felt wretched for her as I disenthralled myself from her doorstep, briskly walked to my car and began the long drive home. I wanted to shout at her to be honest and upfront and surely she would meet someone. And yet I was nearly in tears for her as well, imagining her returning to her lonely quest the moment the door closed, pouring a double for herself as she sat down at the computer and tried for another, declaring that she had once appeared in a "Fly-Me" ad, but please don't count the decades that have intervened since then.

It really was an experience that reinforced why I hated dating as a divorced guy in his late fifties in an age where, for some, sex would be the next move after the handshake and a single drink. Or that, via the internet, you could package yourself to be what you think others were looking for, even though the facade would fall away the moment you truly met for real and not just in some fantasy cyber reality.

Not to say that all of it was bad. I really did meet several nice women, and am still friends with a couple of them on Facebook or we exchange the occasional "How are you doing?" emails. And all now know that I am very happily married and have been polite enough to genuinely wish me well … as I would for them.

Oh, and the site that advertises that, after you take an exhaustive hours-long questionnaire, you'll be connected to your soul mate? I finally tried that one. My soul mate? Out of a radius of one hundred miles, including a couple of major metropolitan areas, the site sent me the profile of a fork-lift operator. Hey, no prejudice against fork-lift operators, really! One of the neatest, most intelligent friends I've ever had was the greenskeeper who was my boss at a golf course in New Jersey. Roy was a friend, a mentor, and a fascinating character who would consume cigars from both ends simultaneously, chewing up one half while smoking the other down to a spit-covered stub. It's just that I had to wonder, what would be the points of commonality with the fork lift operator? And, okay, at least send along one photo please. Let's be honest, appearance and integrity about age are factors out there. If you've been out in the cyber dating world you know what I mean.

I finally gave up on Internet dating.

In fact I finally just gave up. I have a very close friend whose wife passed away fifteen years ago. He only dated one person since then. It was ironic that they had met because she was a fan of my books and I had fictionalized my friend in several books. She had recognized his name when they had first met, asked if he knew me, and from there had dated for awhile. He finally gave it up. His conclusion? He had a twin flame, she was no longer of this world and he was content to wait until they meet again. Poignant, but I so well understand it now.

I did wonder if that person had been Mary of so long ago. I had reached the point of resigning from the game.

And then, at that moment, Charlotte walked into my life.

Maybe you have to stop searching and, only then, will you find what you seek.

Two chapters of back story have now passed. I do

know several extremely successful relationships that were found on the Internet. One of Charlotte's closest friends was matched up with her twin flame on the site with the lengthy test. But for most of us? I bet all who have been out there and are reading this have at least one, "You won't believe this!" story to tell.

My conclusion? It is the face-to-face, eye contact, and all of the subtle nuances of voice, gestures, and body language: the way her eyes look straight into yours, that are all so crucial. Maybe the Internet will bring you to that moment, but until then, do you really know?

I met Charlotte the old-fashioned way, and in that first instant, I knew. The preparation of the soul for the twin flame comes out of all these experiences.

TWIN FLAME

Chapter Five Narration:
Learning Process toward Communication Skills

Twin flame soul-mates are whole souls long before blending with a partner — they do not become whole as a result of joining together. They never merge into one entity. The flames parallel each other in love, support, trust and sharing their lives in equanimity. They accept the individuality of the partner and provide a loving environment in which to carry on the joy of living together. Shared vision in a relationship is found in what is colloquially referred to as a soul-mate. A person who is like-minded, a best friend and loyal companion. If romantically involved, then a wife or husband. Samuel Taylor Coleridge the poet first used the term in 1822 in a letter he wrote to a young lady. Coleridge said, "To be happy in married life ... you must have a soul-mate." He went on to say, "In order not to be miserable, you must have a soul-mate as well as a house- or yoke-mate. Coleridge advised that the spouse be both for marital bliss. How they achieve this awesome relationship involves excellent communication skills. The skill set is learned and varies from couple to couple. The approach and techniques learned are eclectic.

There is a learning process toward communication skills between twin flames and the use of the talking piece is a good place to start. The Native American talking piece is used by many to create an environment within the privacy of the home that provides structure and safety. In one variation on this, the couple sits facing each other. They light two candles, placing them as close as possible without actually touching. There is structure using this ancient technique that suggests while holding the talking piece, the partner is the only one who can speak. The talking piece is selected because it has deep meaning to the relationship so it might be a seashell that they found on the beach during their honeymoon. The talking piece takes on an energy of its own and evokes intense emotion. As the person picks up the talking piece he takes a deep breath and allows the mind to fill at that moment with what he plans to say. There is no preparation for the words, no mental chatter in advance. This enables both to listen more attentively rather than preparing in advance what they plan to say. The extemporaneous nature of this plan creates an intimacy unique to this couple. The words flow from the heart and the partner reciprocates by listening with the heart. The language is sincere, honest and spoken in love. The time frame is limited to a few minutes so there is equality in the dialogue and no one feels that they are being lectured to, but rather true classic communication between people who adore each other.

A short period of meditative reflection will follow the communication exchange. The calming effects of meditation can impact in a positive way both mentally and physically by reducing stress, increasing energy and enhancing mental clarity. It is the perfect modality to calmly relax into focusing the mind's attention on what you want, not on what you don't. Focus the mind to concentrate without interference from other or outside thoughts. This enhances the words taken in from the soulmate.

Few notions will serve people more faithfully than clearly defined plans on how to move forward. Simple ways to solve problems such as the lighting of twin flame candles and expressing themselves fully allows the soulmates more time to spend together doing the things they enjoy. It brings a peaceful coexistence to the marriage by enabling heart chakra communication. A few additional thoughts for enhancing the process might include introspection, goal setting and setting intention. Introspection in a relationship is a necessary step. It reveals things that may need to be corrected, eliminated, energized or strengthened. Fear, for example, is often viewed as weakness, but by applying an approach of non-judgmental awareness you can identify your fears and anxieties, formulate a plan that addresses specifically how you can deconstruct them and reclaim the energy they steal from you.

TWIN FLAME

Chapter Six

~
The First Thanksgiving … Time to Meet the Family

As I write this from the perspective of three years later it fascinates me how memory works: how particular moments stand out so clearly and then behind those moments, there is a general sense of delight with life. Ask me to recall all of the other events that transpired during that time, what happened at work, what was the news of politics, the ebb and flow of life, of what Sandburg called "news of springtime and of harvest time," and those memories become fuzzy and indistinct. But of Charlotte, so much is in sharp focus.

There is an interesting school of thought that postulates that time is relative within our minds. Interesting stuff to contemplate. Each of us has experienced it and, after such moments, wonder, "What is time? Is it always the same? Or is there some strange relativity to it after all?"

Certain events seem to stretch into a surreal distortion of time so that the passage of a moment can seem forever. During a second of time, you can recall a dozen different thoughts. You can recall in rich vividness the most minute details imprinted on your mind forever.

When the topic of time and memory comes up for me, I immediately recall an auto accident when I was twenty-one which I mentioned earlier as a vivid encounter with the protectiveness of my guardian angels. Though this is about my journey with my twin flame, this side note might have merit because it explains something about perceptions of time. It was an event that profoundly shaped me.

It was a spring morning in the springtime of life. I was

driving to school, a road that I would traverse across eight semesters, each semester of fourteen weeks, so I had traveled it more than five hundred times or so each way. Ask me to remember the details of that road and I can barely recall any of it now, except for one place, one intersection, which will always stand out sharply and frighteningly clear.

It was there that a woman ran a stop sign, then, in a panic, slammed on her brakes and came to a dead stop across the entire width of that narrow two-lane country road. I was driving a VW bug at fifty miles per hour. As she ran through the stop sign I registered it, disbelieving, ready to shout an obscenity as I started to hit my brakes. I assumed that she would speed off and I'd skid around behind her, a narrow miss but typical of driving in New Jersey. But then, oh my gosh, she stopped, and I knew there was no escape … and it was going to be bad.

From the start of the incident to impact was most likely less than two seconds.

Those two seconds stand out in memory as interminable. A fraction of a second of disbelief that it was actually happening and then time just slowed down. I clearly recall thinking that I should pull to the right but then realized I'd go into a ditch and most likely roll my bug. Roll an old Volksy? Time to die! They caved in just like a real bug that had been stepped on.

Swing to the left? A telephone pole at the corner of the intersection would slice through my VW like a hot knife through butter and kill me. Remember, VW bugs had the engine in the back. Up front was a fragile gas tank that, when ruptured, would spill fuel into your lap. If there was a hot spark around … I didn't want to die that way.

Then, memory flashed (remember that all of these thoughts are transpiring in the span of less than two seconds) of my father teaching me to drive. He was darn good at it. Beyond teaching all the basics, he drilled into me survival skills when behind the wheel. He told me that if someone was triggering an accident that would be a bad one, perhaps fatal, hit his car! Hit his car!? There were several points of logic in this advice. The other car will absorb energy far better than a pole or tree, improving my own chances of survival. A cold, but pragmatic point. Hit the culprit who created the accident because if you don't, there's a high chance he'll race off and leave you behind with the bill, perhaps to die, abandoned in a ditch while he merrily drives away. New Jersey Survival Driving 101.

All of this was flashing through my synapses even as I was skidding down that country road. My decision? Hit her and maybe I'll survive. During the final fraction of a second, decision made, I aimed for her car and even pulled the wheel to skid in on my right front corner, letting my empty passenger side take the impact, and then I hit. The last flash of conscious memory was my slamming forward, my shoulder harness snagging me, and my glasses flying off my face, impacting the windshield, to later be found in the back well of my car.

I think I was briefly knocked out. The time distortion ended with someone wearing a motorcycle helmet banging on my window and pulling the door open asking if I was okay? How long I was out, I'm not sure. But from the moment I knew I was going into an accident, a bad one, to impact? Two seconds at most? It will always stand in memory as timeless.

The guy in the motorcycle helmet pulled me out of my car. I tried to walk but he sharply ordered me to lie down. My body felt numb. I tried to take a few steps but somehow my right leg wasn't working as it should. I looked down, my pant leg at the knee was torn open, and I was bleeding. Only then did the pain hit. My kneecap had been mangled when it hit under the dashboard and I had a mild concussion. He found my glasses, put them on me, lit a cigarette for me, bless him, and stayed with me until the police arrived.

Now here's the other part that relates to the purpose of this book. I remember a police officer arriving, kneeling down by my side, quickly checking me over, telling me to remain still, and that an ambulance was on its way. He then he asked me a question, "Son, were you wearing your seatbelt and shoulder belt?"

Back then seat belts and shoulder belts had only become standard equipment for a few years. There was still a lot of debate with people claiming it was better to get thrown clear of an accident. Yeah right! My dad constantly harped on that issue for the stupidity of it. Thrown clear? My last conscious memory was of my face coming to a stop just inches from the windshield. Thrown clear? I would have been hanging halfway out of a broken windshield.

But there was something else sinking in, and sinking in deeply at that moment. On that particular morning I had left my parent's home in a foul mood. We had yet another typical fight of a twenty-year-old son who thinks he knows everything, and with parents just about fed up with it all! I had stormed out, climbed into the car, and driven off to school, fuming about how idiotic my parents were and why was I, of superior intellect and understanding of the world, stuck with them and still under their all-controlling thumb? (No memory of course of their helping me to buy the car, helping with my tuition, or the fact that Mom had, as she had been doing for years, gotten up early that day to cook breakfast for me.)

So the officer had asked me, "Son were you wearing

your seat belt and shoulder belt?"

Just a few minutes earlier I had been rounding a bend in that road, about fifteen seconds out from the idiot driver running the stop sign. I was cruising along at fifty, no seat belt or shoulder belt on. I was about fifteen seconds from dying or, at best, having my face ripped off on the windshield glass.

And at that instant a voice spoke to me. If it has ever happened to you, you know what I mean. If it has not happened to you at least once in your life it will and I know it will seem bizarre and you might wonder, is my memory of it just some distortion of recollection created by the accident? It was there within me, that voice, and it was most definitely real, as real as these words that I now see on my computer as I type them. There was a voice within my head, insistent, firm, demanding obedience: "Put your seat belt on now!"

I will swear to that memory until my final breath. It was an urgent order, the type of thing that you just obey without questioning, and maybe later, if nothing happens, you just shrug off to imagination or to the lingering memory of a dream. I had obeyed it, and seconds later that shoulder belt stopped my face from shattering, my chest slamming into the steering wheel, crushing my ribs, and likely killing me.

All I said back was a whispered, "Yes."

I recall his kneeling by my side, looking down at me, smiling with reassuring fatherly hand on my shoulder and then saying, "You're lucky son, you'd have been dead if you hadn't."

I would have been dead? When you are young and only twenty, you tend to feel immortal. And then there it was. I could have been dead that morning. I think I began to cry from the shock of it all. He told me to remain still. I have a vague memory of the guy in the motorcycle helmet and a woman staying with me, trying to divert my attention from my twisted up leg. I have a memory as well of the officer actually exploding at the woman who had triggered the accident, his saying that she could have killed me. She never said a word to me, never a word of apology or even a query if I was going to be okay? (It turned out that she was a cousin of my father's supervisor, who said it was her third or fourth accident like that. Typical isn't it? And by the way, I'm glad I hit her and totaled her car as well. Think of it, a Volkswagen totaling a big old Buick!) I've walked a bit funny from the wreck ever since, but at least I'm still walking.

After the ambulance arrived, they strapped me to a gurney and took me to the hospital. The pain was not too bad, and my thoughts dwelled on that voice and the strangeness of the few seconds before I hit. Then my parents were racing into the emergency room, both of them crying as they hovered around me. I was crying as well, shocked by the thought that I could have indeed died that morning, and that their last memory of me was of a spoiled jerk kid shouting at them as I headed out the door.

So what did that have to do with twin flames? The last thing first: I learned. I learned that never again would I part from someone I loved, or worthy of my love, with such sharp, bitter words. Because maybe, just maybe, those might be the last words ever shared. I don't always live to it, but I try. The other lesson? I do believe in guardian angels.

At home that evening after the accident, I lived and relived the shock of it, talking it out with my parents and a couple of buddies who had come over to see me. But I told only my parents about the voice. Both of them had a spiritual bend to their thinking and view of life. Both of them accepted my account without question. And both of them said it might have been my "Tappy" looking out for me. Tappy was my beloved grandfather who slipped away from this world when I was eight ... and has lived in my memory ever since. Tappy, a guardian angel? Why not? If love is eternal it extends far beyond this transient mortal life and is but an instant in eternity. Who are our guardian angels? Who knows? *Listen to it*!

I've already written about my firm belief that guardian angels helped guide Charlotte and me together. Some might ask, does that fit into a Christian perspective? Absolutely! The appearance of angels, in both Old and New Testaments, happens scores of times. Why wouldn't there be such miracles of guidance for all of us in our daily lives? Some of my friends doubt this, saying that if God is all powerful, why does He need angels as messengers? But, from Lot warning the doomed citizens of Sodom and Gomorrah not to insult an angel, to the angel messengers to Mary and, later on, to angels bringing succor to Christ in the desert, there are numerous Biblical references to angels. If we accept that, why not the gently beautiful miracle of guardian angels in our own lives? Protecting us at times, nudging us along at times? I just hope mine don't take offense to my picturing them as a bit disheveled, perhaps chewing on the stub of a cigar or an old pipe, and conspiring and coordinating with Charlotte's far more lovely angels to bring us together.

Charlotte speaks of how she felt before our meeting, as if something was loudly urging her to approach the stage where I was signing books. It was a push that had no logic or understanding for her other than the fact that *something* was guiding her to meet me. If one accepts that concept, then this world truly does seem like a far better place to be.

Servants of God are all about us, ready to help guide us, even when we are not asking for it.

That incident left me fascinated with the concept of time. It created a better understanding of what Thorton Wilder wrote about in *Our Town*, that few of us ever truly realize how beautiful life is while we live it, except perhaps for "saints and poets," and that so many moments of our lives can be sublimely precious, if only we would open our eyes and our hearts to see the true miracle of being alive. (Performing the role of the Stage Manager in that play, to be able to deliver those few words about "Saints and poets," was a high point of my life)!

When you discover at last your twin flame, time will distort, interestingly in both directions. There will be moments when mere seconds become near endless and yet, underlying that, the days, weeks and months will begin to merge together into a blissful sea of time that truly feels eternal.

Thanksgiving is always an evocative day for me. It triggers childhood memories filled with warmth: waking up to the smell of a feast being prepared in the tiny kitchen of our row home and turning on the television to WOR channel 9 to watch cartoons and then the big Macy's parade in New York just across the river. At around eleven o'clock or so, my dad would bundle my siblings and me up and take us for a long walk up to the South Mountain Reservation. That was a wonderful place filled with memories and fantasies of childhood. The South Mountain Reservation was twenty-five hundred woodland acres nestled into the first range of low-lying hills west of New York City. It only rose up several hundred feet or so, but for this kid it was "my mountain range."

It was rich with history. Washington Rock atop the crest line was supposedly the place where, during the Revolution, General George Washington himself would come to the observation post set up there in order to keep an eye on the British troops occupying Manhattan and Staten Island. It was the place of childhood adventures, where I would play that I was a lonely sentry keeping watch for General George. It was one of the places that shaped me to become a historian and writer.

The traditional Thanksgiving Day hike was so important to me. Not until many years later did I realize what a sacrifice it was for my Dad. With a badly injured back from his time in the horse cavalry during the War, he was locked into a ten-pound brace, keeping him rigid from hips to ribcage. Climbing that ridge and back, every step must have been filled with pain. But he never showed it. Every Thanksgiving morning, he'd push us kids out the door for a two-hour hike to stir my finicky appetite and to get us the heck out of the way of my grandmother, my mother, and my and aunt laboring in the kitchen.

Returning from the hike, dinner would be spread out, ready to be served. Even as a kid I waited for the family tradition to unfold: my mother tasting the turkey. We'd sit down around the table in the tiny dining room. My father would fill each plate and pass it around until all were served. He'd lead us in a good Catholic grace and then the moment of testing was at hand! Always it would be the same as the plates were filled: grace was said, and then my mother would try the first taste of turkey breast.

I'd wait for it as she looked around at us, "It's okay…" A pause, and then, "but not as moist as last year's."

I think by the time I was five or so I was ready with my yearly response, "Mommy you said the same thing last year."

Cold stares of admonishment would follow as I would then chuckle over my plate of turkey and stuffing, muttering in *sotto voci* that if last year was not as good as the year before, then when indeed was the legendary turkey of true taste and ultimate moisture? 1940 perhaps? Or was it 1928 before the Depression or maybe before the First World War? Where, in sacred memory, was that moist, palatable turkey of such gastronomical delight? Or was it all legend in my family, a holy grail never to be found?

Or perhaps the answer was just ahead of me now?

Thanksgiving Day with Charlotte's parents was at hand. Our wild, crazy, passionate courtship was three and a half weeks along. It was time to … drum roll please … Meet The Parents.

A soon-to-be-discovered wonder of our courtship was that Charlotte's parents lived only three miles away from my house, owning a beautiful stretch of woodlands on the east slope of the same mountain that I lived on. Charlotte was still living in Asheville at the time, but she was already building her dream home on five acres below her parents' house.

She came by before noon to pick me up for the fateful rendezvous on Thanksgiving Day of 2013.

Was I nervous?

Hell yeah.

This was Meet the Parents time. Strange, here I was, sixty-three years old and I had a touch of cold feet and clammy hands. The dreaded Meet the Parents moment was at hand. Memory of all of the Meet the Parents moments burned deep within my psyche. Any of you guys reading this with a touch of testosterone in your veins know the feeling. For after all, if we get down to the basic biological aspect of why we like girls, and why the good Lord wired us the way He did, there is something about making babies tied into all of this. And how does one make babies?

Don't ever, ever discuss that with the father of the girl you are dating. In his mind, whether his daughter is seventeen or forty-three, she is his darling baby girl, the one he once played smoochies with, carried on his shoulder, walked hand-in-hand with on sunlit mornings in the park, tucked in at night with a bedtime story and song, wiped tears off of her dirt-smudged face, and kissed her scratched pudgy knees to make them "all better." He would watch with disbelief as one day she would grow up and kiss him one last time on the cheek before running out the door to plant a deep tongue-twirling kiss of lust on some pimply horny guy.

So at sixty-three I was about to stand at the door, to be greeted politely of course, but would dad stare at me, thinking, "You horny SOB, what have you been doing with my girl?" Would mom stare at me, thinking, "My God he's twenty years older than she is! Dirty old guy, my girl needs to find someone her age or better yet, a bit younger." I was about to run the gauntlet of meeting not just the parents but the entire family. Charlotte's twin brother would be there, and, like any proper brother, he had to feel protective about his sister and carefully check out this older guy who was without doubt trying to paw at his sister. The brother's wife would be there, most likely judgmental about a sister who must be crazy to go out with some whacko professor and author. A couple of uncles and aunts ready to shake their heads whispering, "You know these author types. Most likely has groupies all over the place and Charlotte had better wake up. He's just playing her because she's younger and cute."

From Charlotte's side? She was nervous but in the

other direction. Anxious whispers of preparation floated in the car as we drove those three long, very long, miles to the palace of the parents.

"Grant," Charlotte warned. "They're a bit strange. Dad might needle you a bit, don't let him get to you. Mom has Asperser's the same as my daughter, so whatever she says, take it with a grain of salt. My brother, he's okay but he thinks I've got problems. You can't smoke your pipe in the house, is that okay? They'll like you, really!" I sensed that in her mind I would see creatures with two heads, memories of all those satirical movies about holiday gatherings playing out in our reality.

The door swung open to such wonderful scents. I had an instant flash memory to Thanksgivings long ago. Her parents were standing there, mother offering to take our coats, father extending his hand. Make eye contact, my inner voice whispered, solid eye contact, firm handshake, not too hard, not too weak. Keep eye contact even though that first gaze might be an interrogation: Just how far did you get with my darling baby girl last night? Are you already going for a home run you son of a…?

And then there was a smile of welcoming. Charlotte and mother were hugging, Charlotte, so typical of her, headed to the kitchen to help out, and her dad, also typical, handed me a potent martini. Their house, perched on a ridge with an endless view to the east, clear to Hickory fifty miles away, was a place of warmth. Their home was filled with life, laughter, a gathering of kin, three delightful granddaughters, one of them Charlotte's daughter Samantha just home from college, and, something I instantly loved, half a dozen board games spread out on the coffee table and floor.

Their fireplace was huge, the wood burning with crackling warmth that radiated throughout the vast living room. I loved it! I grew up in a tiny New Jersey row home that dated back to the early nineteenth century. There was no historical romance to that place. It was cramped, drafty and, I swear, the entire house leaned ten degrees aft in the rear and ten degrees forward in the front, as if ready to split apart. A fireplace? Actually it did have one, uncovered when I was five or so, when walls were torn out to replace old lead pipes and turn-of-the-century mice- and rat-chewed electrical wires. I was fascinated with that fireplace, once the only heat source for that old house It was promptly walled back up and entombed like some ancient mummy when the repairs were completed. As a kid I thought it kind of strange, imagining people who lived in that house long before I was born hovering around that entombed fireplace during stormy winter nights. Therefore where was the fireplace of my childhood? I found it on channel 9 television out of New York City, broadcasted from a dozen miles away. From Thanksgiving to New Year's the television station, after ten o'clock at night, would point a camera at a real fireplace and that was it. A black and white, twelve-inch wide fire. Really, that was it! The big action, while I would sit and stare, waiting for the moment, was a hand reaching in to throw another log on.

Sure I had fireplaces when I grew up and moved on, something I insisted on, and of course I had one with my house in North Carolina. But it never really felt the same. I had a fireplace, but never really a sense of family gathered around it. Not to denigrate an ex-spouse, but that true feeling of inner warmth and comfort was never really there. I found it, though, on that first Thanksgiving Day with Charlotte's family. The family gathered around as logs crackled, flooding the room with cheery warmth. Within minutes the anxiety of earlier washed away. Some might call it sexist (I would call it traditional), in all the best ways possible: the father of the woman I had fallen in love with was sitting in his oversized easy chair "holding court," drink in hand. Teenage granddaughters were hunkered down over a board game, shaking dice, laughing and arguing, the brother and I were talking guy talk about politics, flying and such, Charlotte, her sister-in-law, and mother were bringing out snacks to hold us at bay until the turkey was truly ready.

The long anticipated moment was at last at hand. The great sacred turkey was drawn out of the oven, tested and probed, and declared ready. Oh great turkey, I always wonder how you and your kindred view Thanksgiving Day? But what the heck? Call it karma for turkeys and may your spirit find a heaven filled with vegans. For me, I can't wait to get at the crackling skin, white meat, and stuffing buried within.

We clustered around a large round table, hardly a square inch of it not burdened down with turkey, sweet potatoes, those wonderful small onions you only see once a year, string beans garnished with nuts, mashed potatoes (I'm getting hungry just writing this), gravy, glasses of wine and cider, and then all of us were holding hands as the pater familias led us in a true prayer of thanksgiving. The first slices were passed around and the "great testing" had arrived ... how moist would this bird be?

I looked around the table ... and waited for it. I've always believed that I should wait until those who prepared the meal were seated and had taken the first bite before I will raise my knife and fork. There were comments to dig in, but I shook my head, smiled, and whispered that I can wait for Charlotte's mother to sit down. I glanced sidelong to Charlotte sitting next to me, her hand brushing against my leg and squeezing it affectionately with thanks for my gesture. All were then waiting for her mother Linda to try the results of days of preparation.

Memories were flashing, my mother's first bite of the yearly bird offering, which was never as good as its legendary ancestor. Charlotte's mother cut a piece, tried it, and smiled, but not too broadly. Being too pleased with one's own work, be it a turkey or an attempt at writing the great American novel, is always a sign of hubris. It was her father Earl's turn to try a bite with a broadening smile.

"Excellent, you outdid yourself Linda."

We all now dug in, loud primal sounds of grunting, masticating and sighs. And oh my gosh, this was truly it!

I was eating the legendary moistest turkey of all times! I looked heavenward. "Mom," I silently whispered, "this is The Turkey, The Turkey you spent a lifetime in search of. Surely this is a sign from heaven that I have found my new home." I think I got a little misty eyed.

The feasting continued: more gravy, more of those little onions, "yes another slice please," another bottle of wine making the rounds. There was laughing and smiles, and an urging on to eat more. All the time, I was cognizant of the lovely woman sitting inches away from me. Our hands brushed, sometimes slipping under the table to clasp for a moment. A glance up revealed her mother watching us and smiling. She liked me! I could sense it in that gaze, obviously happy that she saw her daughter happy. A bonding was now forming with that woman as well, a bonding that would come to fill a void in my life ever since the passing of my own mother. It was a bond that would help me through a very tough time to come. I could sense that if only my mother were still alive and with us at that dinner, how the two of them would be in the kitchen later, whispering together, occasionally giving Charlotte and me sidelong glances, nodding together and then resuming sharing stories about how not so long ago we were still children in that time of a mother's memory that all mothers must eventually let go of.

Dinner was finally pushed aside with groans of satisfaction, someone claiming the living room sofa to collapse on. It must be true that turkeys have some sort of mellowing agent locked within. Maybe if everyone in our country ate turkey at least once a day this would be a better place.

Now it was board game time. I inwardly cautioned myself to be restrained. You see I was, and always will be, a board game junkie. Old Avalon Hill and SSI war games of Gettysburg, and Battle of Britain and that penultimate challenge: Risk. I'm deadly at that one, my normally mild-mannered personality going full-blown alpha, from Clarke Kent to Superman (but a very dark alternate universe Superman who takes no prisoners and chortles at that beautiful moment of betrayal as I wipe my opponents off the board and cast them into the darkness).

Can't do that now! In my best inner soul, "William Shatner school of acting," I kept telling myself, "Must be restrained, must be restrained!"

Nevertheless, an hour later the dark side had taken hold of me, laughing at the anguish of Charlotte's nieces as I stalled their Parcheesi pieces in a blockade, Darkness settled outside and still we played and it was at such a moment that I felt the time distortion kicking in. I looked over at Charlotte, sitting on the floor opposite me, her seductive peek catching my eye and my heart, now trying to melt me into removing my blockade on the Parcheesi board. Temptress! Did I melt? No. Did I love it? Oh yes. That gaze could slow time down to a "saints and poets" moment of being so completely aware of just how wonderful life truly was. It was a moment of realizing simple gifts. The fire was glowing warm, the kids were laughing as Charlotte's seductive appeals to move my blockade fell on deaf ears. My potential father-in-law, Earl, was sipping a good brandy, interjecting comments into the dispute and laughing at his daughters' failed attempts. Linda was making sure that snack plates and glasses remained full.

My blockade was foiled as Earl jumped ahead to victory. Oh well, it was a good move, I tried to rationalize, to always let a potential father-in-law win, while I silently internalized the agony of defeat.

The other side of the time distortion occurred as well. The stretching out into a sense of timelessness where past, present and future merge into one. There is the old joke that God invented time to keep everything from happening at once. At times we mere mortals, in a blessed moment, can capture that reality and float in it. I was part of a family again, floating in the time of that moment but other experiences drifted in, overlapped, and merged. Memories of the walks with my father on Thanksgiving Day, my grandfather Tappy sitting up late with me, the boon of a holiday when I could know the pleasure of staying up until midnight, the two of us gazing at the television, waiting for the mysterious hand to appear to poke the twelve-inch black and white fire and stick another log in, cold, crisp Thanksgiving nights, bearing with it anticipation of Christmas to come.

This year I would know Christmas with a family that Charlotte was offering to me.

The following morning we were up early, her family filled with anticipation because I was offering airplane rides for any who would dare to venture heavenward with me. The day was perfect, no wind, a limitless sky waiting as I opened up my hanger and proudly rolled out my beloved World War II recon bird, an original Aeronca L3B. In the three weeks of our courtship Charlotte had already gone up with me several times. Our second time she even christened herself ... she got airsick.

I pride myself on being a very cautious and courteous pilot. I hate those fools who, once they get their victim in the air, they announce, "Let's see what this baby can do!" and proceed to terrorize their passenger. And besides, someone is going to have to clean up the mess. With our second flight a week before Thanksgiving we started to hit some turbulence bouncing off the mountains. Charlotte finally whispered that she was feeling queasy. I immediately turned back for the airport, trying to keep things stable. Five minutes out from the airport there was a gasp over the intercom from the backseat, "I'm going to get sick."

I told her there was a sick bag tucked into the side of her seat. A moment later a desperate reply, "I can't find it!" And then my reply, a truly stupid male reply, "Use your handbag!" (Charlotte can not go anywhere, even up in a plane, without a handbag by her side). A strangled reply ensued, "No!" (I didn't find out until much later how much those handbags cost!) What to do? I tore off my authentic looking World War II "fifty mission crush" hat and offered it back. Another strangled "No!" A moment later that scent wafted forward. Oh my gosh did she vomit inside the plane? All right, my first thought as the owner of a precious antique plane was, it's okay to vomit on yourself or down your shirt, inside your pocket or up your sleeve, but for heaven's sake don't do it on the floor boards! It can leak through, that acidic substance eating into the canvas body of the plane underneath. It would mean tearing up the floorboards, gingerly scrubbing out the congealed mess and, as any old pilot knows, the stench stays in there forever, wafting up especially on hot humid days, and overriding the lovely perfume of canvas, leather, hot engine, exhaust and aviation gas which, to any aviator, is more seductive than Chanel No 5.

"You okay?" I nervously asked as I opened the window.

"Yeah. I'm sorry," came the feeble reply.

I masked my priorities for the moment. I didn't ask her how or where, I just calmly said that we were going into the landing pattern and would be down in a few minutes. With landing I had to stay focused on my approach as I glided in, gently touched down, and taxied off the runway.

I was able at last to look back. Her features were pale and in her hands she was clutching a clear plastic baggie filled with something that looked like Campbell's Cream of Mushroom soup. God bless her, the woman had managed to find a baggie at the last second. Those handbags! They're better than Batman's belt when it comes to having just the right thing for emergencies having pulled out a ziplock bag at the very last second before loosing breakfast. She was ready to stick it back into her handbag and take it home for proper disposal. Once out of the plane I laughingly took it, much to her embarrassment and which turned to a bit of disbelief, cracked it open and threw the contents out behind my hanger, announcing that it was a precooked meal for some hungry raccoon. She darn near lost it again. But to my delight, she was gamefully ready to fly with me one weekend later and eager for me to share my plane with her family.

With all those extra hands it was easy to open up the hanger. All were standing quiet as I went through my preflight check list, rolled the plane out, put Charlotte in the cockpit when all was ready, and, like so many old wonderful planes, I stood in front of the plane, looked around to make sure all were following the safety rules and standing aft, shouted "clear prop!" grabbed hold of the propeller, and pulled it down hard. Talk about feeling macho and just a bit of a show-off as the engine fired up. My lovely Charlotte was already a veteran of this, and throttling it back to idle as the engine caught fire and roared to life.

It was a moment of music in my heart and soul ... the roar of that engine coming to life, smoke blowing out of the exhaust, the air vibrating with the seductive cry of an airplane throttling up and eager to head for the realm where it truly belonged. Any pilot will tell you that there are airplanes, and then there are *airplanes*! Those seductive beauties that become a part of you, to take you aloft on laughter silvered wings and open the heavens and the clouds above you, where together you turn and toss and weave in the skies that were once only the realm of hawks, eagles, and angels. My twin flame already knew that about me, and, I would come to learn, was not jealous of that plane, but instead loved me even more for the love I had for it.

I put on my hat as I slid into the pilot's seat, the soundtrack from that incredible scene in *Band of Brothers* when the vast air armada begins to lift off to face their "Day of Days," echoing in my mind.

On this day of days, I was taking my potential in-law family aloft. Was I showing off? Hell yes! Her father was out there, camera in hand to record it all, as Charlotte first went up with me to prove it was all safe, circling the grass strip airfield as we climbed heavenward into that bright blue November sky. We finally nosed over into a low pass down the runway, followed by a sharp pull up, leveled out, and then came in to land.

"Who's next?"

What a delightful few hours as first her daughter, then her nieces and then her brother went up with me, to circle, wing over, swoop, and touch the heavens. Flying for me is part adrenal rush and part spiritual, the place to indeed reach out to touch the face of God.

I drifted in to land, filled up with a load of aviation gas, and then hangered the plane. Everyone was beaming, especially Charlotte, for it was obvious that she was showing off the man who was becoming the love of a lifetime. And what fun for me! Every time I take up a newbie and introduce them to touching the heavens, not in an aluminum cylinder cruising at thirty-thousand feet, but instead flying the way it used to be, in a wonderful old four-cylinder plane, bouncing along a grass runway to lift into the sky, wheel and bank, swoop and climb. To hear their laughter, that is a blessing.

We tucked my beloved bird back into the hanger. Charlotte was already calling her "the mistress" but without jealousy. (Years earlier I briefly dated someone who accused me of caring for my plane more than for her. Guess what, she was right! And this book is definitely not about her). If someone can not understand my love of flight, to appreciate it without jealousy, and in fact urge me to go up whenever I am feeling glum, that someone could never be a twin flame. The twin flame in your life should understand what you love and, even if she doesn't embrace it herself, smile indulgently when you go forth, and you feel eager to return to her loving embrace.

We left the airport in her dad's oversized SUV. Her parents, brother and wife and their two delightful daughters, Charlotte and I started the long trek up into the mountains north of the airport. The mountains, which at that time of year become the destination for tens of thousands seeking a precious Fraser fir.

The Christmas trees at the street corner stand in New Jersey, magical though they were to a child, were, in more pragmatic memory, scraggly things. I can remember one year when my ever-patient dad bought two of them, cut off the branches of one malformed fir that must have been raised downwind from the Route 1 oil refineries, drilled holes into the second tree nearly as malformed as poor Gollum, and then glued the additional branches into place. Of course they wilted and started to fall out by Christmas evening.

But we in North Carolina have the corner on the Christmas tree capital of the world: thousands of acres of true, blue-green Frasers. It was a cold, windy day as we spilled out of the SUV, family splitting off in several directions, disappearing into the vast grove of trees carpeting the steep hillside. The air was rich with the aroma of Christmas, mingled with the scents of wood fires, hot cider, and chocolate simmering, an offering to those in search of that perfect family tree.

Charlotte and I wandered off hand-in-hand together, a hundred feet into that grove and were quickly lost to view. And yeah, we were in each other's arms, hugging, already engaging in that lovers' babble that makes the other smile, but, oh heavens, if others heard they'd shake their heads and whisper, "There they go again." Frankly we could not keep our hands off each other, if not holding hands we had our arms around each other!

We wandered this way in that wooded paradise because it seemed now that any place we were together had a touch of paradise to it. We heard excited calls; a tree had been found! What a fun family ritual it was, the search for the family tree. If one is an impartial observer of a family upon such a quest, one can nearly instantly pick out the personality types. Is dad the indulgent one with still a touch of the wide-eyed kid in him? Is mom thinking about the thousands of needles to be swept up, or how the tree will sparkle on Christmas morning and fill the house with the intoxicating scent that we all associate with Christmas? The kids, be they two teenage nieces or forty–somethings, just want the biggest tree possible.

The owner of the farm cut it down for us. Even if you have to drive a couple of hundred miles, on that one special day of the year, go to where they are grown, especially if it is a chilly November afternoon, the woods around you already cast with long shadows by three in the afternoon.

The tree was bundled up, needing several of us to push it up onto the roof of the car, butt end and tip jutting out over the front and rear. You see, their house has a twenty-foot ceiling and Earl always wants that tree to nearly touch it, its ever-widening branches spreading out nearly ten feet to either side.

We drove down the winding mountain road in late afternoon twilight and finally up the long driveway to the family home. A family home that I was being invited into. Of course, I was providing an extra set of arms and back to haul that nearly twenty-foot tree through the back door and into the living room. The historian in me could not help but visualize shades of Iwo Jima as, together, we hoisted that tree heavenward for its one final stand, to then be decorated and honored, and to create yet another season of memories.

Mingled in with that evening of raising the tree and adorning it with the family's treasured decorations came so many other memories for me. The sad little trees that my father had cobbled together to try and make one look whole ... how I loved that tree, feeling that it was somehow special and, because of its deformity, I should love it all the more. There was a tree that my brother, sister, and I had carried home on a snowy evening, a gift to us from our landlord who kept a Christmas tree lot behind his hardware store. Then there was a tree on a Christmas morning after a great Christmas Eve blizzard. The roads were all closed, my mother to her final days remembering that day with warm tears of nostalgia because that was the Christmas morning we walked to church and back, "just like in the old days," she would say. Memories of Christmas trees with my grandfather because his birthday was Christmas Eve. I always felt so sorry for him, worried that he didn't have a happy birthday because it was all overlapped by Christmas. I would find some little gift, a trinket from the Woolworth's five-and-dime store, or some other offering, wrap it myself and put it under the tree for him and make sure he received that gift on Christmas Eve.

And then there was a Christmas tree when I was five and Tappy had my first train set ready for me, but not under the tree. It had been a labor of a grandfather's love for me, constructed and worried over down in our basement, next to the coal bin, access to it blocked off by a big sign on the basement door, "Grant Keep Out!" What a Christmas morning that was when, after the sign was removed I first raced down to the basement, and then, wide–eyed, came up to sit under the tree to find all sorts of things for my new train set: railroad cars and a locomotive that actually blew smoke and little plastic trees to set in the village that he had made for me.

Then, a poignant tree of Christmas … the year that Tappy died. I set a small gift under the tree in memory of his birthday.

Memory and time when you are in love, all can flood together into a whole, becoming part of a river that flows gently on, some moments stretching into eternity, others drifting by, buried deep within, an inexorable mysterious journey that your twin flame brings alive within you. And if you are blessed, you are aware of it all in those moments. You embrace it and thank God you have been given the gift of that moment.

Thus it was with Charlotte and me, that first Thanksgiving shared with her, shared with a family that brought me in through their doorway, embraced me, and said, "Share life with us and thank you for loving our daughter." I shed more than a few tears across those blessed days, days which have become part of the treasured memories of my life.

TWIN FLAME

Chapter Six Narration
Root Chakra

Love, as it was meant to be, is first learned in the early years from the family. All of the good, bad and sometimes unpleasant root chakra issues emerge. Our early years set the tone for what we hunt for all our lives. The root chakra is known for basic instincts and survival needs such as food and shelter. The early family years can create open root chakras, allowing a healthy twin flame partnership, or an imbalance resulting in negativity and insecurity which keeps the adult functioning in survival mode around the clock rather than a trusting person needed to enter any relationship. The Chakra system is a Sanskrit belief that there are spinning wheels emanating from nerves in the spinal column. There are seven chakras that correlate to the endocrine system and even come complete with theories that each chakra is associated with a color. It is believed that if the chakras are open and clean spinning and a person is not losing any energy, that disease processes are unable to permeate the etheric level and attack the human body. The root chakra is located in the area just below the waist and relates to the medulla and produces the flight versus fight response. All basic survival instincts come into play with this chakra. There are ancestral memories imbedded in the root chakra of trauma from ancestors. The color affiliated is deep red.

The life of a child revolves around the loving nurturing parents and the extended family of aunts, uncles and cousins. It is the first and last time a utopian environment exists and many people spend the rest of their lives looking for the same safe place or, at the very least, attempting to recreate it. Within a few years after birth the toddler is disciplined and meets with the first series of disapproval and restrictions from the caregiver. A few years down the road the young child watches the adults he adores disagree, fight, and act without morals or ethics. It is a confusing and scary time. The human frailty and character defects become apparent and young teens begin their journey to recreate the early years of absolute trust and faith in humanity. They yearn for the joyful life of the childhood, before they witnessed the relatives exhibiting greed, jealousy, arrogance and addictive behaviors.

It is part of the soul's journey now to find someone like himself or a life partner with similar vision. The search begins and fails in a quest that includes serial monogamy in various relationships and sometimes the attempt to find the twin flame by getting married to the wrong person. The insight that finally happens for some is that, put simply, they need to work on themselves. The soul connection that they yearn for only comes after looking inward and accepting themselves with love and self compassion. Karuna: The primary key to romantic relations is authentic loving relationships with all of humanity. The spiritual connection of the soul-mate progressing to twin flame explodes with the realization that if they had remained in the toxic marriage their real purpose would have not emerged.

The end of toxicity in relationships allows the more authentic self to emerge so they can complete the spiritual acceptance and understanding and work more on who they were meant to be. This permits the awesome opening for a twin flame to enter, the one true love of this lifetime and eternally with "the one." This opening is a different vibration from past insights; it is at the level of souls spiritually emerging and telling each other in every way that this is "the one" we have both been waiting for. The one person who is there to teach and learn respect and experience joys and sorrows with. The prepubescent spirituality of the early years of existence on this earth is replaced by a profound maturity of awakening. It includes self love, compassion and loss of fear. Our interpersonal relationships are the most important part of our lives. Complete attention to one's own needs is a dead-end in terms of a happy, useful life and often eventuates in addictive behavior, which is a dead-end in terms of attaining any degree of maturity or happiness. Love means, among other things, the willingness to put the interests of another before our own.

If Socrates was correct when he said that an unexamined life is not worth living, then it is also true that a human life without at least one meaningful human relationship is not human at all. If we choose not to or cannot develop a meaningful, mature relationship with at least one other person, we exclude the most satisfying experience any human can have. However, even if one agrees with all of the above, it does not automatically follow that we will ever establish an intimate, meaningful relationship with someone. This is because a mature relationship requires serious and sustained effort that many people seem unwilling or unable to make. It's fascinating that the animal kingdom is again more advanced with black vultures, French angelfish, bald eagles, turtle doves and even the albatross mating and remaining monogamous for life! Putting another's interests above our own is difficult for a prolonged period but that is exactly what must be done in order to nurture and develop a mature lasting relationship. Relationships depend on love and love is a gift, freely given. We may choose to accept or reject is. We may desecrate it or we may nurture it.

At the end of our lives our relationships will, in large

part, determine the meaning and success of our lives. If we have ignored our relationships and do not nourish them or attend to them, then we have in many ways failed in life's most important purpose. To die lonely without having had a sustaining human relationship at least at some point would be to die a mutilated human being in a way. Nothing is more integral to a meaningful human life than a mature, loving relationship. And nothing provides more happiness and satisfaction. Developing a loving monogamous human relationship is worth all of the effort expended and provides a degree of fulfillment in our lives that nothing else can.

Anagrams help us decipher the mystical symbolism in words. Prairie Voles mate and are monogamous for life and the anagram, vole=love.

Chapter Seven

~

The Time of Troubles

Earlier in this book I've alluded to a major speed bump that awaited Charlotte and me. During the time that it happened it was absolute hell for both of us but now, in retrospect, it was a time that had to be endured in order to test the mettle of who we are both as individuals and as a couple.

When you meet your twin flame later in life you cannot help but be carrying baggage from the past. For, after all, long before you met your twin flame, you had met someone else and possibly married her. You got married to a person who, at the time, you had thought, "This is it," or maybe it was, "I think this is it." This is not the time or place to analyze the choices that Charlotte and I made long before we met. It is definitely not the place to denigrate whomever it was we chose to be with, especially when it comes to the person with whom we chose to have a child.

Sufficient to say that at some point in those relationships there came a terrible moment of realization, "My God, did I make a mistake?" And eventually a tragedy unfolded. There is a myth out there that a divorce can be an amicable situation: both of you are adults, both of you finally realize that it simply is no longer working, both of you decide to shake hands, and, for the sake of the child, you think you can part in a friendly manner and go your separate ways in life.

It is never that simple. For one or both there is too much hurt, even in the friendliest of departures. Inevitably it will get ugly and in so doing will leave scars that can hurt for a lifetime. Or, even if not married, a relationship haunts and can leave wounds that continue to ache and create fears of what lies ahead.

An analogy from a military historian. Studying war is part of my business and perhaps comparing love to war is not all that far-fetched, for, after all, both reach deep into primal emotions. I've interviewed hundreds of veterans from World War II and studied the history of the Civil War in depth. A good example of comparing love to war might be that of the famed Civil War general, Winfield Scott Hancock.

He was a magnificent leader. At Gettysburg he commanded the Union troops that would face Pickett's Charge. He led from the front, an officer who, without hesitation, exposed himself to enemy fire and did so recklessly in order to inspire his troops to make a heroic stand. When that gallant but foredoomed Confederate charge came straight in at him on the third day of the Battle of Gettysburg, he unflinchingly rode along the front line, shouting for his men to stand. Just as Pickett's brave men were falling back in retreat, the moment that the "high tide of the Confederacy" began to ebb, General Hancock suffered a near mortal wound. It was an agonizing blow close to his groin that left him bedridden and near death for more than half a year. It was a wound from which he never fully recovered, physically or spiritually.

Returning to action a year later, he rode into his next battle ready to face the storm yet again. His veterans looked to him again for inspiration. "Hancock the Superb," as he was known both by friend and foe, was back on the field of action. The bullets began to hum around him. Rather than brace up in defiance, gaze fixed upon the enemy, calling for his men to follow his lead, he began to flinch, and was seen to actually be shaking, his features gone pale. No one, before or after, ever doubted his courage. He would serve through the rest of the war with distinction, but never again was he the "Gallant Hancock" of old, ever eager to ride along the front of the battle line to inspire and rally his troops. No one would ever dare to question his valor, for he was "Hancock," but never again would he gallop along the front lines, heedless of risk. The memory of the pain, the agony of his near fatal wound preyed on his soul and courage to the last day of that war and for the rest of his life. No one ever would doubt that he was still a man of courage. But only those who had truly experienced the pain he had endured knew just how deeply it could scar a man long after mere flesh had healed.

Courage is like a well, for some it goes deep, for others the water is shallow, but for all it is finite and can eventually run dry. Too much pain, and even the strongest will thereafter shake with fear, though his heart still struggles to be strong.

The same is true when it comes to the ability to completely trust another with your heart and soul. Wounded badly enough you might never be able to "go out there" again. We all know at least one tragedy like that, a person hurt so badly in a relationship that even if he does start to date again, the ability to truly let go and jump into what I call "free fall" is now beyond him. Caution, like a rope wound around the heart will, for the rest of his life, keep him bonded to his fears.

There is often a dual tragedy there. The inability to truly let go of his fears and love without hesitation becomes a barrier to someone who does have the ability to love fully and without restraint and offers that kind of love to someone who has been wounded far too deeply. The one offering love, tragically, often comes out of it doubting who he is, asking himself what did he do wrong … and perhaps is then wounded as well.

It is breaking through that barrier of doubt that is perhaps one of the biggest challenges of all for twin flames.

Charlotte and I both carried "baggage" from our prior relationships. Yet again, this is not the place to cast blame upon those in our past. Undoubtedly, if those from our past might one day read this narrative they would have more than enough negatives to offer and some undoubtedly have merit. A tragedy that lingers as so many relationships end is that one or both wind up hurting the other to, as the saying goes, "aim for the jugular." We try to justify some of those actions but rare indeed is a relationship terminated where both can say, "The other was a really nice person, but we simply weren't made for each other and we realized it was time to move on. There are no regrets and we still are friends."

So yes, I went into this relationship with my twin flame with baggage, as did she. Both of us had crossed through a chronological demarcation line, the magical three years that so many marriage counselors and wise old ladies give advice about. For both of us it had been well over five years. There really is something about that three-year mark from a divorce that is valid. Time to heal, time to let the inner seas of turmoil calm down, time to regain self assurance, time to try trusting again, both yourself and the other.

For Charlotte and me, more than a year had now passed in our relationship. Charlotte had a ring on her finger (from a pawnshop in Asheville, not Tiffany's, an offer she had refused when we were in New York City on a business trip). But did we both start to have anxieties? In quiet moments, especially when alone, absolutely yes.

Remember the story of General Hancock? Undoubtedly, months after his terrible wounding, he would publicly say he was ready, even eager to get back into action. But what about at two in the morning, awakening sweat-soaked from dark dreams of fear and pain, the memory of that terrible instant where the bullet had slammed into fragile flesh, tearing a bloody path that tore his soul as well. To then awaken and indeed there was still real pain, physical and spiritual that would linger for the rest of his life. Did he lie in that bed, alone, fearful and shaking at the mere thought of facing "it" yet again? He would not have been human if he had not endured such fears.

A year into our relationship I began to hear from Charlotte a phrase that at first I'd smile when she said it, and laugh dismissively. She would say, "I keep waiting for the other shoe to drop."

Anxiety was creeping into her soul. "He's too good, too perfect. There has to be something wrong with all of this. *There has to be!*"

The deep well of all our fears awaited to swallow up the dream.

The dark well of our fears. How deep that truly can be and how destructive it can be. Now add into it all the chatter of the world around us.

We live in a tragic culture. What happened to the wisdom, learned across thousands of years, that some things should be sacred? I grew up during the turmoil of the 1960s. The rise of a culture that for awhile was called the "me generation." That if you were not out there "doing your own thing," you were missing out on life. Pledge yourself to a life-long monogamous relationship? The cultural wisdom became that you were passé, missing out on life … and besides could you ever actually trust, I mean really trust, the other person to fully adhere to such a life as well?

As I lead into this chapter I cannot help but rail against those on the outside watching a once-in-a-lifetime relationship begin to blossom. There is always someone standing on the sidelines, ever ready to whisper words of fear. "Do you really know him?" "How can you really be sure?" Or the one I truly grit my teeth over, "You know, I heard from someone who has a friend who knew him and she said..."

Have you ever been called in by your boss who closes the door, sits you down, shifts a bit uncomfortably, picks up a sheet of paper, and then starts with, "I'm uncomfortable with this, but someone here has filled a complaint against you, saying that you said..." You respond with, "It's not true and I'd like for you to call that person into this office and have him repeat the same lie in front of me." The response? "Oh I can't, this was given to me in confidence..." And thus it begins.

I had several such incidents in graduate school, stabs in the back from what are now called "social justice warriors," out to end the academic career of a graduate student who, being politically conservative, did not fit their view of being politically correct. At least in that world I knew how to fight back. I would not sit back passively, to be dragged before a star chamber inquiry, not even knowing who was accusing me of some "thought crime." The best response? "Next time we meet, my lawyer will be with me and I am filing counter charges of harassment and violation of my Constitutional right to face my accuser." That always sent them reeling backwards.

But when it comes to your relationship with another, when you are hearing whispers of doubt? Even if you shake it off with a response of, "I've known her for a year now, I trust her completely, and tell your friend that unless she wants to repeat what she said in front of both of us she can go to hell," it can still haunt and tug at your inner fears. For, after all, were you not ultimately hurt by someone long ago whom you thought you could trust and did not listen to the warnings of others?

No matter how bright the flames of a twin flame, sooner or later memory of having been wounded by another long ago, the whispers of someone who claims to be well-meaning, one's own self doubts, the drumbeat of a culture in which monogamy and lifelong love is a concept that many now scoff at or claim is impossible to find, will keep one awake at two in the morning.

The doubts begin to intrude. A month after the giving of the engagement ring, it was briefly returned for a week but then we reconciled. Illness began to intrude as well. On one side, a rare medical condition. Charlotte had a small tumor on her pituitary gland, benign but nevertheless interfered with proper hormone flow. Several doctors misdiagnosed it as not requiring surgery and then gave her a prescription that in rare cases can have profound emotional impacts, the medication chemically similar to of all things LSD. It would eventually come as a shock when digging into the nature of the medication doctors had been pushing her to take, to find patient accounts of how that medication had driven some beyond despair and radical mood swings, compounded by the malfunctioning pituitary gland. It would not be fully resolved until after the "time of troubles" that I am now writing about, requiring going through several specialists until we finally found a true gift from God, a surgeon up in Boston who had pioneered a surgical procedure that could remove the tumor in less than two hours. But that would be in the future for us, first we had to get through the stormy time in our relationship.

While Charlotte was dealing with that medical issue, along with the at times nagging and intrusive comments of one alleged friend in particular who was dead set against our relationship, I was wrestling with a high stress career.

Being an author, as already mentioned, is so often stereotyped in our culture. Authors are either leading a life that seems filled with excitement and adventure, a bit of the Hemingway fantasy of living life large (it isn't true and recall what living that lifestyle finally did to Ernest), or on the other side the stereotype of the neurotic locked away in a dingy smoke-filled office. This is partially true. If there is an occupational illness for authors it is substance abuse.

Unlike most of the work world you don't have to get up at seven in the morning, shower, shave, be sober, and coherent. It is instead a thirty-foot commute from bed to coffee machine and then to office. You can spend the day in a funky old shirt, unshaven, and turn out brilliance. Or at least try to. And when it doesn't flow, especially at two in the morning, maybe, just maybe, a little lubricant starts to appear. And as the years and the books pass, more and more lubricant can flow. I'll confess that a couple of times I have danced around the edge of that cliff, especially when critics were piling on and I was dealing with a real jerk of an editor while working on a coauthored series (not my current team who are a pleasure to work with!!!), who at one point informed me that I was "just a cog" in the publishing business and that uncooperative authors who didn't buckle to his controlling demands can always be replaced with a more pliant author eager to obey even when he knows the editing and marketing input is dead-on wrong. It can be a brutal business. The warning flag for me, though, was how many authors I knew who had fallen into the pit.

A potential relationship killer? Oh yeah. I recall

attending a science fiction convention many years ago and was single at the time. I was having breakfast in the green room and noticed an attractive women sitting with a friend. We made eye contact, and a smile was exchanged. Hm, I thought, get up to fetch a cup of coffee behind them, then say hello and see what happens! I headed over to the coffee machine, got diverted for a moment by someone wanting to talk, turned, and the mysterious woman was gone. I asked my friend, "Who was she?" My friend laughed and replied that yeah, there had been that eye contact moment, a question from her of, "Who is he?" When informed that she was flirting with an author the response was sharp and to the point, "I dated one and I'll be damned if I ever date another," and she got up and left.

Dating authors is a hard chore at times! And it gets really bad in my case when I am "in the groove." I tend to be a binge writer. I might go for several months staring at the ceiling, playing chess, or just surfing the Internet, but when a book hits, it hits to the exclusion of nearly everything else. It can get so intense that some years back I had an understanding with my doctor that once I turned a book in, I went straight to his office for a full checkup and then a couple of weeks of rest and "vegging." I've worked a lot of jobs in my life, including construction and golf course greens-keeping. Writing a book is even more exhausting.

So can this impact a relationship? Big time. The pleasant routine of courtship is suddenly on hold, "Sorry honey but I've got to write tonight." It can become obsessive compulsive. She's had a rough day, wants to talk it out, but I am staring off, inner mind running through the plot point of a minor character, life and death decisions inside my head as to whether to bump him off or can that character play a role five chapters down the line? It might seem amusing or even endearing for awhile, "Oh, he's creating his next book." But after awhile that can turn into "Yeah, he's still working on *the book*."

Charlotte was facing the downside of being in love with an author.

I could sense that the "gears of our relationship" were still meshing together, but at times grinding a bit out of synch with each other. But it's only for another six weeks or so would be my reply, and then months of free time to enjoy, before the next book comes along.

And then a real bump hit.

It was November, a year into our courtship. I was surfing the Internet while taking a break from writing and saw an article about an upcoming solar eclipse. Usually they are in some exotic location on the other side of the world and out of my reach, but the one for March 2015 would skirt the east coast of Iceland and overlap with my college's spring break. Wow! I've always wanted to check out Iceland anyway, given that another passion is seeing the aurora borealis, which had been a commonplace experience when I lived in central Maine, but absolutely rare for North Carolina.

I excitedly mentioned it to Charlotte. March? She shook her head. Charlotte is a CPA and March is her nightmare month and she replied with, "Why don't you get a couple of your friends to go with you?"

Sure. Why not? She said it was okay. Before the night was out I had enlisted three buddies for a guy trip to exotic Iceland to chase an eclipse and maybe catch the northern lights.

I have a friend who long ago recruited me to go on an archaeological expedition to central Russia (where we got arrested by the old KGB) and from there to several expeditions to Mongolia. (There are moments when an author actually can have some real adventures!) My archaeology friend used to say that, "A man should always have an adventure ahead of him." He was right. The moment I booked the Iceland trip, I felt that tonic of adventure flowing through me. Yeah, it is a bit of a testosterone thing, a trip with the guys to a foreign land to chase an eclipse.

Finishing up the book I was working on, which had diverted me for months, and impacting big time on my relationship with Charlotte, the trip to Iceland was all I could talk about at times, as guide books and maps came in, technical articles about eclipses and northern lights, a television program about weird food and the cuisine of Iceland with rotting shark fins and, dare I say it, whale meat.

It was not registering that I was marginalizing Charlotte. Hey, we're twin flames, everything is cool, our gears are meshing nicely, she has the ring back on. I was not reading the warning signs, that she was internalizing the anxieties, not so much about the trip but all of the anxieties about a relationship that inner voices and a couple of external ones were whispering had gone too fast.

She drove me to the airport and I was way too much, "Hey diddle de di, it's the adventurous life for me!" And at least one alleged friend was whispering to Charlotte, "Four guys off to Iceland with all those hot-looking Nordic girls waiting…" I did sense that subtext a couple of times and tried to point out that two of the three traveling buddies with me were Anglican priests, one my spiritual advisor for more than a decade who was recently married with a child on the way.

So I was off to Iceland and she went back and put on the chains to her computer and the fun world of being a CPA for the four weeks before April 15th.

Two days later I was in Iceland on a guy adventure. Now there are guy adventures and then there are guy adventures. This one was definitely the former. Two Anglican priests, both of them happily married, and a straight-arrow buddy whom I've known for thirty years rounded out the team. Did we get a bit riotous? Sure, especially our third night out when the sun cooperated by exploding with the largest geomagnetic storm in nearly a decade, triggering a massive display of northern lights that blew across the heavens from horizon to horizon, so intense they were clearly visible even before the sun had fully set.

It was a freezing cold night, but the hotel we were at had a sauna which our hosts heated up for us. I stood outside for fifteen minutes shouting, "Oh, my God!" as rainbow-hued arcs of light blew from horizon to horizon, then I peeled off my coat, ran into the sauna for five minutes, then back out again. After six hours I was so chilled that when I finally retreated to my room I was shaking uncontrollably for an hour. It was then that I called Charlotte and rambled on nonstop about just how incredible it all was. Given the five-hour time difference there she was still chained to her computer and well, I was not really listening back to what she was doing and feeling. It didn't help that I had sought some internal warmth with a few too many shots of vodka as well.

The next night it hit. The moment she answered my phone call I could sense that something was amiss. The conversations which once flowed with such ease and warmth simply were not there. If there was fault maybe I'll venture to say that she was not openly expressing the feeling that she was being marginalized, and on my side I was not fully listening. But after that conversation a full-blown anxiety attack hit me.

By the sixth day or so my phone calls were filled with anxiety. "What's wrong?" Reply, "Oh, nothing's wrong." A deadly routine was beginning to settle in, filled in by the long-ago memories of getting wounded and memories of the wounds lingered on, even though inflicted in lifetimes left behind.

By the time I flew home and was met at the airport, I could clearly sense that something was indeed amiss. Anxieties on both sides had taken hold. I still saw her as my twin flame but something was going wrong.

Things quickly came to a head. And what was the root cause? Perhaps old FDR summed it best when he declared that, "We have nothing to fear but fear itself." We both were becoming afraid of the other. Afraid of just how badly we could be hurt. Afraid of what might happen. The sum total of those fears transcended all the happiness we had shared and had believed would be the reality of this life and what would come afterwards.

And it was compounded by the ministers of fear. A voice whispering that it had been a nice "affair" but do you really truly know the other? Think of the age difference! You know statistically he might very well up and die long before you and then what? And the real killer, "Maybe this isn't what God intended for you after all. Less time with him and more on your own might be healthy for you right now." Add in a medication with a side effect never discussed by a doctor, add in the stress of work, for even when not writing there is a lot of stress tied to marketing, interviews, and planning yet another book.

It all hit like an avalanche, a true tsunami a week or so later. Charlotte came to my house and without preamble handed back the ring, said it was really over, then clearly stated I was not to contact her or come to her house ever again. She turned, got into her car and drove off. An hour later I violated her injunction, driving to her house to appeal, only to find it locked up, darkened. She had disappeared ... literally. I stood in her darkened driveway in numbed shock.

Thus began The Time of Troubles, as we would come to call it.

What I am writing next is without doubt the hardest part of this book. Remembering it now still sends a wave of anxiety through me. Most of what I'll describe is a compression of the facts.

My world died that day.

I returned home, stunned, unable to react or act. The following day I reached out to her parents. I told them what happened and asked if they could at least locate her so that I knew she was safe. Hours later they came back to me with word that she was holed up in a hotel sixty miles away. A hotel? Why?

A very crucial point to now make regarding what sustained both of us through this Time of Troubles. Both of us had made a pledge, before God, of our fidelity to each other, that we had entered into a monogamous relationship that would be lifelong. There was no "exit clause" in that agreement other than absolute truthfulness to each other.

Perhaps the only criticism I shall level to what transpired in my life before Charlotte needs to be voiced here. I had been on the receiving end of affairs. No details on that other than the fact that it had hit me as a devastating shock. That was one of the wounds I carried across the years and into the time when I first met Charlotte. In our first months of dating, when Charlotte initiated the conversation as to what was happening in our relationship, and what it meant for the future, she forever stilled any further anxiety about that issue. She had pledged monogamy to me, as I did to her. If we were broken apart, forever, I trusted her enough on that first terrible day to tell me the truth. On the one hand, if someone else was coming into her life, she would be totally honest with me upfront, and not drop the bomb on me after the fact as had been delivered to me before.

And second, if she thought a future between us was totally dead, she would release me from my pledge to her. But I had already resolved that whether our twin flame soared up again or not, I would remain faithful to her for the rest of my life. Sound extreme? Not at all. I had no desire to be with another and knew that if ever I did, it would only result in hurt and a lie. Perhaps the most painful thing ever to endure, or to inflict on another is to be with her and wish it were another. I knew I would always wish it was Charlotte and she would later confide that such were her feelings as well. If she could not be with me, she did not want to be with anyone else.

Thus the news that she was holed up on a hotel, though disturbing in the extreme, did not raise the specter that she had run off to enter an affair. That simply was not, nor ever would be, Charlotte. Yes, there was anxiety. I did know of at least one friend of hers, who from the beginning of our relationship had lurked in the shadows, and whenever possible had tried to spread seeds of doubt. My few encounters with this friend had been tense, in one case simply walking away rather than react. It would come out that he had indeed encouraged her anxieties.

On my side? I only confided the full story of what was going on with four people, two of them my closest friends, the third her mother, the fourth a personal counselor with whom I had been talking for several years. All of them were people with a very deep faith in God and all of them knew the qualities of Charlotte's character. Why just those four? Because I trusted them and they knew Charlotte. Not once did any of them even remotely suggest that someone else was in the picture. I knew some others with a more cynical attitude would only stoke the fears that could eventually come to drain away my trust or encourage me to say, to hell with it and just go out and date another. The refrain of that old and frankly disturbing song, "If you can't be with the one you love, love the one you're with." Perhaps there is a key lesson there in a time of crisis? Turn to those with deep insights, not just into you but into the other person as well. Turn to people with a well-balanced sense of spiritual faith. The twin flame phenomenon is tied to that, above all else. It is something that transcends the physical of this world and comes to you from a deep and profound place.

Though broken apart two things stayed clear to me, even when my world felt shattered and at times a deep depression would take hold. Though broken, I trusted Charlotte to remain truthful to me. Second, from the beginning I carried a faith that God would guide us to what was right, and my innermost thoughts and prayers told me that we would eventually reconcile. And yes, I prayed like I had never prayed before, I mean on my knees type of praying. My prayers were always answered with the same response, "Trust in Me, continue to pray and all shall be well."

And so I did trust in Him for four long and very painful months. Perhaps the hardest thing to do in those first weeks was to observe Charlotte's injunction. We've all been through painful breakups, on both the initiating and receiving end. Even if the breakup is with the best possible intentions, meaning, "I'm sorry but it just isn't working out for us," someone is going to get hurt and at times hurt badly. Having been on the initiating side of this type of thing, I absolutely hated to see the pain the other was going through. Regardless of the reasons for the breakup, to inflict pain is the last thing one wishes to do to another. There were with some the agonizing tearful phone calls, the showing up at my doorstep weeping, and even a few situations that were uncomfortable with the other pitching a fit.

I knew that an open emotional appeal would only exacerbate the fracture that was already there. And beyond that, it would inflict more pain on Charlotte. I knew in my heart that she still loved me. What purpose would it serve to stand at her doorstep in tears and appeal for a return? If she "broke" and agreed, what would be the ultimate outcome? Or, worse yet, she came back because she pitied me, or did so because she simply could not bear to hear my appeals and see my tears. No matter how much a test of one's will, never do that to the other, it will always end badly. I found patience and prayer to be the best possible answer. There had been inner anxiety on her part as she tried to go through the motions in a relationship she feared might be flawed. On my side, there was inner anxiety as well that it would blow open yet again.

"Trust in Me, continue to pray and all shall be well." I had to hang on to that. If Charlotte and I were indeed twin flames, it would work its way through. And I knew something else. This was a test. It was a test of our deepest faith in each other. Yes we were broken up. But was it not, as well, a "fiery trial?" If in the state of being apart we continued to hold true to certain values, certain truths that we professed to believe in, was that not part of this process as well that maybe all twin flames need to go through at some point in their relationship?

I look back upon that Time of Troubles now and, as with all painful events in our life, my mind and heart draws a curtain, Call it an anesthesia upon the anguish. Memory of pain becomes dulled and healed with reconciliation. Was it really that agonizing? Hell yes!

One factor that made it even more difficult to adhere to her request that I refrain from going to her place to launch appeals was the simple fact that we lived just three miles apart. Her route into our village passed just below my house. Did I at times find a reason to head into town at a time when I knew she might be on that road? Yeah, I did. I was forcing myself to observe her, "Don't come here, don't call me," order. But a passing by each other on the road? It happened more than a few times and both of us would admit later how our hearts skipped over and tightened at the sight of the other.

My friends ... how I must have driven them to near distraction. I fell quite hard at times, especially in the middle of the night, lying awake, staring at the ceiling, awakening in the morning where for a few more blissful seconds reality had yet to hit. It was most painful when I dreamed about her, the dream so vivid it was real, that we were together, talking, laughing, sharing. And then the harsh cold reality of coming awake to a world without her. It was days like that in which I could hardly make it to a decent hour before opening my phone and calling my two most trusted friends for solace. How many hours they stood by my side with encouragement is beyond count and God bless them for it. They were guardian angels in the flesh.

Four long months passed. It was her mother who started to become proactive in this crisis. What a remarkable loving woman she is. My mother had passed away more than a decade earlier, and from nearly the first time Charlotte's mother and I met, I felt a profound bond with her, in so many ways like the bond with my own mother.

Her mother was and is a dream "in-law." Think about that term, it means you are, in a legal sense, bound to another. With Charlotte's mother it was a bond of the heart. We both loved the same girl, but beyond that I knew she loved me as well and would often say, before, during, and after this crisis that she believed Charlotte and I were truly meant to be together.

She did not take sides in this one, but she did offer solace and counseling to me, and in my times of depression worried about me to the extent of showing up at my doorstep with a meal, sitting me down to make sure I ate, and then patiently listening to me. Perhaps that is a component of twin flames as well, that extended families come to recognize the special bond and do all in their power to help fan that flame and cause it to burn even more brightly.

It was her mother who raised a significant component in this crisis ... a medication I mentioned earlier ... bromocriptine. Charlotte had been on the medication for several years due to a situation with her pituitary gland. It is one of only two prescriptions specific to a particular condition. For over 99% of the population it works to varying degrees, though it never actually cures the situation, it only controls it. But in a small percentage of patients it can trigger profound mood swings and even personality changes.

All medications have their downside. One personal example: I've wrestled with smoking all my life. At least since I've met Charlotte I've dumped cigarettes and stayed with a pipe. Being totally off would be better, I know. Some years back my doctor prescribed Chantrix to try to give me a boost with kicking the habit. We all know those annoying prescription drug ads where they show the patient happily enjoying life while a cheerful voice chimes in that the medication being advertised does have potential side effects including the potential desire to want to boil your children's pets on the kitchen stove, maybe boil your children as well, or everyone's favorite disclaimer, "If it lasts more than four hours, call your doctor."

Well, with Chantrix, it was about fifteen years ago, the ads even then were saying it might trigger suicidal thoughts. Not to worry, I thought, that was a rare one, at least that's what the drug company said. From day one I didn't like it, fifteen minutes after taking it I got the shakes. There was no change in my desire to smoke but I reasoned that maybe it will take a few weeks. I didn't last a week. I awoke one morning feeling really bizarre, almost as if still in a dreamlike state. I was staring at my high ceiling and had a clear vision of how easy it would be to attach a rope to a hook … and just hang myself and be done with it.

What the hell!? A minute later I was in the bathroom flushing that damn drug down the toilet and from there to the phone to yell at my doctor. I learned from that to mistrust all medications, check them out carefully before taking, and be hyper aware of potential side effects.

It was Charlotte's mother who really started to jump on the issue of the medication with the instinct of all good mothers saying, "Charlotte has been with me over forty years and this is simply not her. Something else is wrong."

And yes, it was a factor, a huge factor with a lot of nasty side effects. As her mother and I dug into the research we finally hit on some obscure medical journals and a couple of patient commentary pages describing horrible side effects. The scary discovery for this historian? A chemical analysis that the medication is derived from an ergot. Ergot? What does this have to do with my knowledge as an historian? A bizarre mania that frequently hit villages in medieval Europe was known as "ergotism" or "St. Anthony's Fire." An ergot is a mold that grows on improperly stored rye, a chemical by-product, a cousin to LSD. Yeah, psychedelic LSD. Enough of a chemical crossover existed between ergotism and the current medication that in a small percentage of the population the chemical can trigger profound mood swings. Not 1960s style "freaking out" from a bad dose of LSD, but still enough to be of concern. I knew it was not the root cause of the crisis Charlotte and I were in, but it was an obvious contributor.

A side note of frustration over medication side effects and our "factory system" of medical delivery with which we are increasingly stuck. Shortly after our Time of Troubles, Charlotte and I went to a specialist at Emory University Hospital to get a new evaluation that we hoped would lead to surgery to remove the growth on her pituitary gland. The entire day-long visit was an exercise in frustration: records misplaced, schedules messed up, labs not ordered. It culminated with a doctor finally running into our room, where we had waited for an hour and half beyond the scheduled time. A glance at the records and she urged Charlotte to go back on the medication. We were both stunned. I mentioned the research on the ergot connection of the medication. The response? A sharp glance at me with the query, "Are you a doctor?"

It just so happens I am, in history, said so, and raised the studies that a side effect was similar to ergotism. I was cut off with a dismissive glance and the advice continued to simply go on the medication for another year and see what happens. Charlotte was in tears as we left. It was a long four-hour drive home with her questioning, should she just give in? I had already found online a patient commentary page about the medication and started reading off statements, including some where the confused patients were openly saying they were contemplating suicide. So this stuff was and is dangerous.

There is a happy ending to this one aspect and also a lesson: to take control of your own treatment, especially in the face of uncaring, time-stretched, or egotistical doctors who forget the paradigm that we hire them to help us and not just submit to being another number. Charlotte finally found Doctor Laws, a remarkably compassionate specialist up in Boston. She submitted her case to him and, two weeks later, his assistant was on the phone with both of us for nearly an hour reviewing everything, and setting an appointment for two weeks hence. The surgery took an hour and a half and within twenty four-hours, Charlotte's life truly took a new turn. So thank you, Doctor Laws!

After the failed visit and rotten treatment at Emory they actually tried to bill us for eight thousand dollars more than what was agreed upon and had already been paid! They finally backed down after a sharp statement that we refused to pay and would take legal action against them if they pressed the issue. Enough said on this aspect of our Time of Troubles!

A little over three months into our Time of troubles, her mother was finally able to reach out and get her to step down from taking that medication and drop it. A bit of advice to all of you seeking that twin flame. Know and understand all aspects of what medications the other is taking and be hyper vigilant.

A few months before the trip to Emory, there did seem to be a thawing of the long standoff. Charlotte found a few excuses to call me. One rather poignant and obvious one was a photograph of an unusual cloud. As a pilot I have to be well-versed in weather and clouds, what forms them and what they might be a portent of when flying near them. Up here in the mountains we get high clouds that actually look like flying saucers triggered by soaring updrafts rising off the surrounding mountains. She sent a photo of such a cloud and it triggered a few hours of texting that for awhile I thought might open things up ... but then it shut down again. Another encounter occurred shortly after that, again a few hours of conversation, even a shared hug and kiss but then a backing away.

It finally came to a climax late in July. I awoke that morning with a strange sensing that something was about to happen, and then here is the really mystical part of it all. My closest confident called me, all excited. She said she had been praying, then mediated upon our situation and an answer had come to her which was startling clear. Today was the day!

My friend, who can be very alpha when she knows she is right, basically ordered me to go over to Charlotte's place, tell her how much I would always love her, and we would there and then be reunited. Her voice was almost like that voice I described earlier, the guardian angel that had saved me when only seconds away from a potentially fatal auto accident. Listen and don't ask why.

I did stew and pray over this pronouncement for six long hours. Around two in the afternoon I started to nerve myself up. I took a long shower, shaved, and dug out some clean clothes. The physical toll on me of the previous four months had made me something of a wreck so I wanted to look semi-presentable. I kept staring at the clock, counting down the time. Shortly before our breakup Charlotte had taken a part-time job as a companion to an elderly woman who lived further up the mountain. I knew that on Sundays she usually stayed with this woman until five. I did not want her to come home from that and find me sitting nervously on her doorstep. It got to around just before four and I could not stand the stress of waiting any longer. I got into my car and started to drive towards her cabin, deciding that I would first go to her parents' home to talk it over and hopefully get some encouragement.

I arrived at their doorstep and we sat down on their porch, I nervously blurted out my friend's message and my resolve to follow through on it. Both were hopeful, but nervous for me. And it was at that exact moment their phone rang.

What happened next is not fiction. It was real and yet another proof that a twin flame relationship is a special spiritual gift.

Charlotte was on the phone, I could hear her voice. Her mother was talking to her, making wide-eyed contact with me and then replying, "Yes, yes, no he's not at home, he's here … Yes, yes I'll tell him to wait."

Her mother hung up, looked at me and then whispered, "She called from your driveway. She's at your house and she's driving here and wants you to wait for her."

The ensuing three or four minutes were a mixture of exaltation and then outright fear. It had to be one of two things. Had she gone to my house to tell me, that it really was, and forever after, over? Or was my friend right when she declared that this would be the day of reconciliation?

I heard her car coming up the long driveway and it was coming fast. And as with my accident of so many years ago time distorted again, each second of what happened etched like an eternity into my soul. She slammed her car to a stop behind mine. I was standing in the middle of the driveway, trying not to show my fear. She all but jumped out of her car and flung herself into my arms, sobbing that she would love me forever.

I would learn later that her mother, standing at the window, wept as well, as did my friend when I called her later that day to tell her what happened with her uncanny, remarkable prediction.

The following day Charlotte insisted I go with her for a drive. It was a long one of a couple of hours, our destination she would not reveal but I sensed what it would be. We arrived at an outdoor chapel, perched on the side of a mountain, with magnificent, God-inspired views. There she took out a small box, opened it, drew out our engagement ring (she had tried to give it back to me when we broke up but I had refused to take it), and with both of us in tears she asked me to put the ring back on her finger, and then together we prayed to God in thanksgiving and asked for guidance that our twin flame would burn even brighter than it had before.

The Time of Troubles was over.

TWIN FLAME

Chapter Seven Narration:
Disharmony

It starts with minimal differences of opinion or preferences. The pasta is overcooked and he likes it al-dente. She has to remind him to take the clothes to the cleaners which he passes on his way to work. "Is it too much to ask?" is the first combative step in questioning compatibility. Why doesn't he pay as much attention to me as he used to before we started living together? Why does she max the credit card each month and never think to budget or invest? They used to make love all night and sleep half the day, but it is now time to go back to the reality of the real world of working the jobs and paying the bills. Her travel time to the city commute to corporate work precludes the leisurely brunches they so enjoyed during the early honeymoon phase of the relationship.

So, let the fighting commence. In the true fashion of marital discord it escalates to a high pitched rumble in less than a month. Didn't Grandpa tell us never to fight about politics and religion? Well, the heck with that sage advice — the intense debates surpass those of television's political pundits! She is far to the extreme; he more moderate. Are they learning to move more toward the middle in compromise? Not a chance, at this point they will hold strong in their core beliefs until hell freezes over. People bring to the union the sum total of their early years, the combined DNA and environmental influences from their respective lineages. Couples bring their own idiosyncratic fears and preferences for strawberry ice cream over chocolate and liberal versus conservative. If the parents raged over politics the children will also ... but not always in the political parties that their parents adored!

TWIN FLAME

Partnership brings out that mirror image of blaming the other or projecting onto the other person the very character defects they themselves possess. The only way out is to grow at this point into a more self-actualized adult or run. Classic soul-mates endure this verbally combative phase but slowly see themselves as geometric compliments. They emerge on the same side of the coin, respecting differences. They enter the polling booth knowing that the partner's vote will cancel theirs and hold hands on the way out. How will this evolve?

Chapter Eight

~
Getting Married

We got married. We had reached that beautiful reconciliation, prayed together at the chapel, declared to each other that our love was eternal and thus started to plan for The Day.

Something happened though, three days after our reconciliation that shook both of us to the core. I was home working. We had plans to get together later in the day. My phone rang and what unfolded were five minutes of pure terror and a lot of contemplation and prayer afterwards.

The call was from Charlotte. Her signal sounded distant, strange. All I could hear her say was "I'm okay. I've been in an accident." I could hear voices, someone shouting "Lady! Are you all right?!" She was crying and blurted out that she was on the interstate and then her signal clicked off.

I was out the door, running to my car and I could hear sirens. I live close to the interstate and whenever there is an accident I can hear the first responders racing to the scene. This time they were racing to Charlotte! I charged down the hill, not sure exactly where she was, and turned the wrong way. Sirens were getting louder as I drove along a road parallel to the interstate and there saw an ambulance heading in the opposite direction. I pulled a 180, started the other way to get to a nearby entry ramp and caught a glimpse of a fire truck, police cars, lights flashing, and an ambulance tearing along the interstate.

Frantic, I tried to call her. No response. I reached the entry ramp to the highway, tore down it, flooring my car. I could see the emergency vehicles straight ahead.

In crisis we do tend to appeal to God. I was begging Him that it was nothing serious. After all we had been through, why this? A flash memory of my own near-fatal accident. I pulled onto the shoulder and now finally saw her car. It was up off the interstate, backwards, buried into bushes and trees atop the berm, precariously leaning to one side.

My God, what happened?

Pulling up behind the police cars I jumped out and started to run. An officer saw me, came running towards me, putting out his arms wide and calling for me to hold it. Why was he stopping me? What was he trying to hide from me? I was already in tears.

I shouted to him that she was my fiancée, but still he stopped me. I seemed to recall that he actually grabbed hold of me and restrained me from going to her.

Why was he stopping me? What was he trying to hide from me?

"Her name's Charlotte, she's my fiancée, please let me see her!"

The incredible blessing of living in a small town now came to the fore. Everyone on that crash site were locals, the police, the fire department, the ambulance crew. The police officer recognized me, I think he even said my name.

"She's okay! She's okay, they are just checking her over."

Was he lying? Was it worse than he was saying? Someone else came up, I can't recall who, a policeman, a fireman? In my book of life, in this book now, they are all guardian angels for Charlotte, and for me.

"She's okay, doc. Really, just give us a few more minutes to check her out."

Doc. Kind of my other name in my town, being a professor at our college. A couple of the "angels" were old students of mine. How long I waited, I can't recall now, I was so frantic. Fifteen seconds, three minutes, an eternity? And then I saw her stand up, officers and emergency personnel surrounding her by the fire truck. The officer stepped back and I ran to her, the two of us embracing and crying. She was blurting out she was sorry, sorry for everything. I was crying, holding her tight, still terrified, shaken to the core as to just how fragile life truly was.

The ambulance crew was already packing up. They smiled and nodded. I hugged a couple of them, thanked them, and then I started to hear, "She was lucky," "God was looking out for her," "She's okay, just get her home so she can relax." One guardian angel lingered, a man who had been driving behind her and had witnessed the accident and we began to talk.

What happened? Charlotte had merged onto the highway, an entry ramp that both of us have driven hundreds of times. A car that was in the left lane did not see her and began swinging back into her lane. All Charlotte could recall: she saw the car cutting in front of her, its right rear about to clip her left front. She slammed on her brakes, swung on to the shoulder and then completely lost control of her vehicle, a top-heavy SUV. It went into a 180-degree spin, running backwards down the interstate, finally aiming for the shoulder and grass.

The guardian angel who had stopped then said something chilling. "I thought I was watching someone who was about to die." He went on to explain that she was going backwards down the interstate, her car swerving, a tractor trailer in the left lane trying to avoid hitting her and he thought she was about to swerve into that truck and get crushed beneath it. Or across the median into oncoming traffic. And then, it was like God had a hand on her. She swerved back off to the right of the highway, shot across the shoulder again, off the road, then up the side of the berm and into the trees.

As her vehicle came to a stop he was already out of his, running up to her. It was his voice I had heard in the background when she called. He had another comment though that was truly anger-provoking. He told me that the guy who had cut Charlotte off had floored it and fled, leaving in his wake a potentially fatal accident. Coward. There, at that moment, I was talking with someone who was the best of what we are, while the worst had run and hid, not looking back to see if he had just killed someone, thinking only of himself.

A state trooper showed up to interview both Charlotte and our guardian angel witness, and he took measurements of the skid marks. As he was measuring off the skid marks tracking her spin and reverse ride of fifty yards or more, I made a comment to him that, "She had been lucky."

He looked at me and replied flatly, "God was looking out for her."

It was an evening of somber reflection. A reminder of just how fragile life is, how in an instant all can change in such a frightful way. It was a positive reflection as well, a reminder to embrace every moment of happiness with which you are gifted. It was, yet again, a strong reminder, especially after our Time of Troubles, that every moment of life is a gift.

A side story. As an historian I did a lot of work with World War II veterans, of which, sadly, there are so few remaining. There was a common theme I learned from all of them. Having confronted the fragility of their mortality at eighteen or twenty years of age, believing that they would not live to see their next birthday, at times believing that their lives were being measured in mere seconds that seemed to stretch into an eternity, they learned the truth of the beauty of love and of life.

One, a good friend of mine thirty years back, had become something of a mentor for me in my early days of becoming an author. He was such a fabulous guide and motivator. He told me to stay the course no matter how frustrating it was as I tried to climb out of the ghetto of paperback writing. A day came when his wife called me with horrific news: my friend was out of remission and his time was numbered in weeks, perhaps a few months at most. I did not even know he had cancer until that moment.

I went to see him for what I knew would be the last time. When he came out of his house to greet me and led me to a favorite place to sit in his garden next to a racing stream, my friend who had been so robust and full of life just a few months earlier was now so obviously slipping away.

I began to cry. Rather forcefully he told me to stop and then said he wished to share a story.

Back in the terrible winter of 1942 he was serving aboard a tanker filled with high octane aviation gas, traversing U-boat infested waters, bound for England. The tanker was nothing more than a huge bomb waiting to explode. And when it was hit by a torpedo it did explode. My friend was the only survivor, blown off the deck into the freezing Atlantic. Against all odds, a destroyer captain spotted him, disobeyed orders to never slow down, and the crew fished him out of what would have been certain death in those frigid 35-degree waters on a cold November afternoon.

Here was the message from my friend. Against all

odds he had survived all but certain death twice in less than ten minutes. The captain who rescued him gave him a message that he carried for over forty years, to one day convey to me. "Your life has been given back to you, now live every day like the gift that it is."

"Live every day like a gift."

My friend smiled at me as I stopped crying and he took my hand. "Grant, I've had a gift of more than forty years, let's be thankful for that."

That moment with my friend changed my view on life forever. It connects me as well to *Our Town*, about living life fully aware to be a "saint or poet." And it helped to shape my deeper understand of what a relationship with a twin flame is based upon. It is a gift from God.

The months after our reconciliation and that frightful accident, Charlotte and I began to plan our wedding, or should I actually admit that she planned the wedding and I just nodded my head in agreement. I no longer care about any accusation of my being sexist. After decades of elite trying to force their concept of societal norms down the throats of the rest of us, more and more of us are just saying to hell with it, call me what you want, but this is how I really see it. And this is how I see the ritual of a wedding day:

Weddings are more about women than men!

So I went to food tastings, dessert tastings, florists for quotes on flowers and garlands (oh my gosh, can those get expensive!), who shall arrange the music, who will take the photographs, vendors for the invitation and what it had to say, how many can the reception hall at my college seat, then, given that number, can we invite Uncle Joe and we can't ignore cousin Susan who will have a fit but there's not enough room … You men reading this know what I mean.

Talk about stress! Add into this, another tax season was at hand for Charlotte and I was struggling to focus and meet the deadline for another book. So there were "stress fractures" at times!

We had both been married before, so this was not like our first go-around and being, a lot older, we absolutely took any burden of this off of her parents so it was in our hands entirely. I began to think that maybe the rumors were true: planning a wedding is society's way of putting the couple through the ringer, and, like so many rituals that society demands, an entire industry that fuels our national economy was at our doorstep, hand stretched out for yet another check into the thousands.

I was happy to do anything for Charlotte, so with each step deeper into wedding planning I'd just smile and say, "Anything you want is fine with me."

And yeah, the response started to become, "Sometimes I don't think you're really into this. How do you really feel about this flower arrangement for the tables?"

I won't write down the truth here as to how I felt since she is helping to write this book as well.

All I really did care for, with all the falderal aside: I just wanted her wedding day to be the happiest, most memorable day of her life. Months passed with all of this hanging over us. We were three months out from the wedding, which was to take place in my college's beautiful chapel. It was time to pull the trigger and put in the orders for invitations, garlands, flowers, food, location for the wedding party the night before, plane tickets, etc. The logistics were nearly as complex as the plans for D-Day.

And on the morning of March 28, 2016 she looked at me and said, "Let's elope."

Elope??? I laughed (a bit of nervous hysteria in my

voice). "Sure, yeah, let's elope."
"Grant I'm serious, let's chuck it all and elope!"
"What?? Are you serious?"
"Grant, *I am serious*!"

Twenty-four hours later we were at the county courthouse. It was a somewhat aging structure, typical of rural North Carolina with paint peeling from twenty-foot high ceilings. We stood in the narrow corridor into the office of the county clerk who stood behind the counter, grinning (and who, after the ceremony pulled out a copy of one of my books to autograph)! The wedding party? Her parents and my close buddy who had been by my side throughout the Time of Troubles. We filled out the paperwork, checking "no" to the box asking if we were "first cousins or other near kin," (you've got to love the South!) then crossed the hall to the county magistrate who was wearing a heavy metal t-shirt and had just returned from lunch. Two minutes later we were, by the laws of the fair state of North Carolina, married.

Married. Strange, I didn't feel any different. You see, I felt married to Charlotte on the day we had met and knew then that it would last a life time and across whatever awaits us beyond.

Chapter Eight Narration:
"Katallasso"

The wonder of the reconciliation is an inevitable outcome for twin flames. They reunite for the final phase in a joyful and brilliant understanding of who they love, first and foremost. This is accomplished as soon as the gestalt goes off during the split with the partner who left, and who now moves forward to make up. The power to affect this reunion resides with the one who walked out — no amount of candy, flowers or dialog from the dumped one will be effective. There are times when both partners come to the same insight on the same day, because as we know, twin flames are in sync and their vibrations are felt by the other from the etheric tube. Many energy workers, for example reiki masters, feel the cords that connect the partners and the spinning of the chakras when love is the dominant force. Both partners at this point pray for God's will that they can find the way back to each other. The motivation of true love is such a powerful force that nothing at this point will alter the course of a twin flame union.

The gestalt light bulb going off in the mind of the partner who left confirms and authenticates the valuable understanding that the one who walked out is just as miserable as the one who was left behind. During the weeks and months of separation the one who was left convinces himself that he was never loved and falls into deep despair, but so does his partner. If in fact this relationship is a soul-level merging and was meant to be, they move out of this phase of despair and begin to truly miss their loved one. The pull is toward the good memories, the joy of knowing another human who truly loves and adores, irrespective of the arguments about trivial complaints. The separation affords them time to clear their minds and allows the heart to open and soften to these four things: conciliation, communication, commitment and compassion. The 4 Cs of twin flame power.

During the early days of separation the partners go to their corners and initially experience a sense of finality that things will now improve, that the partner who initiated the disharmony and single life will restore a sense of well being. If put on graph paper it might look like a bell curve — the level area representing the less than happy marriage, then a huge surge up to curve into the exhilarating joy of finally getting it right and leaving that relationship which is the key to a happy existence. Within weeks of lunches with the girls, going to movies that the partner hated, and doing all those sushi dinners with acquaintances who were expected to create an idyllic life, reality sets in. She isn't enjoying them quite as much as she expected. In fact they lack substance, and conversation is at best superficial. He can't understand why sitting with the boys drinking beer and yelling at the football game doesn't bring him the same joy as holding her hand on the sofa and eating popcorn while watching an old movie they both just love. Love. If we postulate that true love is shared vision in relationship, that must be the force that drives them back to questioning the choices and behaviors that drove them apart. Rather than accepting the common early days of separation with the thoughts of, it never could have worked, they now question whether this life is any better. The huge spike that created something resembling a bell curve now deflates and levels back down, this time several centimeters lower than where it began.

The curve now moves downward in an inverse bubble that pushes each partner to bottom out and finally come to terms with the meaning of true love. It is a process that involves the memories of the very essence of what created their partnership in the first place. The endless hours of the joy and fascination with the other soul-mate. The process might only include a few of the 4 Cs or all of them, but the outcome is always the same with twin flames: they re-enter the relationship with the intention set to change the various character defects realized during the self-actualization process and recognize the moral virtue of reconciliation to the twin flame love.

In Eastern tradition the Lotus Sutra teaches that there are voices that right speech incorporates. There is a wonderful voice that opens the door to permit the impossible to become a reality. It is spoken like a calming melody, that resonates with the listener a sense of deep compassion and healing to the core of the soul. Another voice that comes with equanimity explains the global interrelatedness of humans. It defines Avalokitesuar as "the one who looks deeply into the world and hears the cries..."

When we feel understanding, suffering is diminished. When we accept that the other is truly understanding our thoughts words and deeds, trust emerges that love exists. Then there is the voice of noble speech and it is a training in impartiality. It includes love, compassion and joy with the impartiality required to experience right speech. Finally, omitting competition between yourself and your partner assures the listening skills and self-compassion that enables the longevity of a sustained reconciliation. Mindful speech is constructive and allows for a peaceful communication that includes good listening.

Reconciliation is establishing a mutual respect between the angry and disagreeable partners, which comes from within. It is heart-centered and emerges when the separated soul-mates cease thinking that the relationship is hopeless, and start praying for and meditating on the idea of how to reconcile. This conflict resolution is best described by the Greek word katallasso, meaning to be reconciled to one. On the day the lighting bolt strikes with this insight it catapults the partners to proactively pursue the process. A calming demeanor emerges and they feel at peace with the decision and commitment to reconcile and again become one.

Conclusion

The honeymoon was a transatlantic journey from New York to England aboard the Queen Mary 2. It was a deeply emotional moment as the ship cast off and made its stately way down New York harbor. As we passed Ellis Island and the Statue of Liberty there were tears, thoughts of my beloved grandfather Tappy, arriving on these shores a hundred years ago, my own journey now a bit of a full circle and carrying within me memory of who he was. I could feel his love, that of my parents, and was filled with warmth that I was embarking on a journey, at last, with my twin flame.

Embarking on a journey. Actually, Charlotte and I have always been on that journey together. The years of this lifetime up until the moment we met were a preparation to more fully embrace the gift we were about to receive. Part of the realization of how precious your twin flame truly is, is to know how life was before you were joined together. To be able to differentiate between that which is of the moment, versus that which is immortal. For true love truly is immortal.

From an Eastern point of view, I realized that as Charlotte and I fitted our lives together, it really was about the yin and yang of existence. That each fits into the life of the other, bringing to you the aspects, both realized and hidden, that round each other out into a greater whole. From a Christian point of view, of so many quotes from the Bible, the one that stands most clearly is the pronouncement from God that He knew us before we were even formed in the womb. If so, that means the journey of eternity for each of us existed long before we were ever formed on this earth, brought into this world to be loved and shaped by our parents, to journey on, to make mistakes along the way, to at times love, or at least think that you love another, to be driven by the quest to find that mystery of a true twin flame, and then to finally be given a true blessing.

How is it that the moment you meet your twin flame *you know* at that instant or maybe it finally does come to you in the days, weeks and months afterward? This is *different*, it is beyond anything I have ever know in this life.
It is as if you have been reunited with an old, old friend, who, at the sight of her after so long apart something surges within you, a reconnection, a *reunion*.
Your twin flame is a reunion. It is proof that love is a gift from God. It is indeed…
Eternal.

December 4, 2016

William R. Forstchen

William R. Forstchen is the author of over forty books, has a Ph.D. in history from Purdue University and is a Faculty Fellow at Montreat College. His broad spectrum of writing includes science fiction and fantasy, historical fiction, alternate history, several scholarly works, numerous short stories and articles and near-future thrillers ONE SECOND AFTER, ONE YEAR AFTER, THE FINAL DAY, and PILLAR TO THE SKY.

www.onesecondafter.com
www.dayofwrathbook.com
www.spectrumliteraryagency.com/forstchen.htm

Books by William R. Forstchen

ONE SECOND AFTER
ONE YEAR AFTER
THE FINAL DAY

PILLAR TO THE SKY
WE LOOK LIKE MEN OF WAR

Lost Regiment series
RALLY CRY
UNION FOREVER
TERRIBLE SWIFT SWORD
FATEFUL LIGHTNING
BATTLE HYMN
NEVER SOUND RETREAT
A BAND OF BROTHERS
MEN OF WAR
DOWN TO THE SEA

Star Voyager Academy series
STAR VOYAGER ACADEMY
ARTICLE 23
PROMETHEUS

ICE PROPHET

A DARKNESS UPON THE ICE
INTO THE SEA OF STARS

The Gamester Wars series
THE ALEXANDRIAN RING
THE ASSASSIN GAMBIT
THE NAPOLEON WAGER

Novellas, available online
"Doctors of the Night"
"Day of Wrath"

With Newt Gingrich
THE BATTLE OF THE CRATER
VALLEY FORGE
TO TRY MEN'S SOULS
PEARL HARBOR
DAYS OF INFAMY
NEVER CALL RETREAT
GETTYSBURG
1945

With Raymond Feist
HONORED ENEMY

With Greg Morrison
CRYSTAL WARRIORS

Star Trek: The Next Generation
THE FORGOTTEN WAR

Magic: The Gathering
ARENA

Wing Commander series
ACTION STATIONS
FALSE COLORS
FLEET ACTION
HEART OF THE TIGER
THE PRICE OF FREEDOM
END RUN *with Christopher Stasheff*

Nora D'Ecclesis

Nora D'Ecclesis is an American bestselling non-fiction author, best known for her international #1 bestseller, The Retro Budget Prescription. Nora holds post-graduate degrees in administration and education from Kean University. Her books focus on stress reduction and cover topics ranging from Haiku poetry and Zen meditation to time management, gratitude and equanimity. She enjoys kayaking, hiking and skiing. Nora lives with her family and dogs in a suburb of Philadelphia, Pennsylvania.

Nora's published non-fiction books include Amazon #1 bestseller HAIKU: NATURE'S MEDITATION, which received the 2017 International Book Award as a finalist in Eastern religions. Her international #1 bestseller, THE RETRO BUDGET PRESCRIPTION, held the top position of Kindle downloads in business/self-help for over a year. It focuses on the importance of tithing to a church or charity and describes in systematic detail how to write a personal budget.

Nora's career has taken her into a more holistic approach

including presenting events and seminars in the United States and Canada. She conducts spiritual retreats based on the her system of health and spiritual awareness. Her books, and seminars focus on wellness and stress reduction techniques. She speaks and listens from the heart chakra in order to enhance communication skills and always includes teaching the techniques of the Native American Calling the Circle using a talking stick.

http://www.onlinebookpublicity.com/tick-borne-awareness.html#.WVbjChPyuRt
https://www.facebook.com/NoraDEcclesis/
https://twitter.com/DECCLESIS

~

Books by Nora D'Ecclesis

TRANQUIL SEAS: APPLYING GUIDED VISUALIZATION
REIKI ROUNDTABLE
MASTERING TRANQUILITY
THE RETRO BUDGET PRESCRIPTION: SKILLFUL PERSONAL PLANNING
I'M SO BUSY!
LOCK YOUR DOOR
THE RETRO BUDGET JOURNAL
HAIKU: NATURE'S MEDITATION
ADULT COLORING: BE A KID AGAIN!
EQUANIMITY & GRATITUDE
TICK-BORNE

www.ingramcontent.com/pod-product-compliance
Lightning Source LLC
Chambersburg PA
CBHW070059080526
44586CB00013B/1123